MEN & WOMEN

Royal Festival Hall
on the South Bank

Poetry Library

Royal Festival Hall, Level 5
London SE1 8XX
Telephone: 0171-921 0943

Books may be renewed by telephone

Date due back

17 JUL 2002

The Spirit That Moves Us Press was the first to publish a collection in English in the U.S.A., by the 1984 Nobel Laureate, poet Jaroslav Seifert—before his award.

We have been publishing poetry, fiction and visual art in a wide range of styles since 1975. We do not promote or identify with any schools of writing or art, but we favor work that expresses feeling, or in some other way engages us.

Individuals and libraries may gain a 20% discount off our titles, and free shipping, by subscribing (ISSN 0364-4014). Please write for our catalog.

Libraries may order direct or through Baker & Taylor, Blackwell North America and others, and may subscribe direct or through Faxon, EBSCO and others.

Bookstores may order direct or through Bookpeople, Inland Book Co., Small Press Distribution, Baker & Taylor, Bookslinger and The Distributors.

The Contemporary Anthology Series

No. 1 *The Actualist Anthology* (indexed in *Granger's*)
No. 2 *Cross-Fertilization*
No. 3 *Editor's Choice* (1980 edition; indexed in *Granger's*)
No. 4 *The Spirit That Moves Us Reader*
No. 5 *Nuke-Rebuke*
No. 6 *Editor's Choice II*
No. 7 *Speak To Me* (in Swedish & English; Spring 1989)

The Outstanding Author Series

No. 1 o.o.p.
No. 2 *The Poem You Asked For*, by Marianne Wolfe
No. 3 *The Farm In Calabria*, by David Ray
No. 4 *The Casting Of Bells*, by Jaroslav Seifert (1984 Nobel Laureate)
No. 5 *How In The Morning*, by Chuck Miller

Other titles:

Mozart In Prague, by Jaroslav Seifert (in Czech & English)
Eight Days, by Jaroslav Seifert (in Czech & English)
Here's The Story (all fiction)
Men & Women

The Spirit That Moves Us is a member of the Coordinating Council of Literary Magazines.

THE SPIRIT THAT MOVES US PRESS
Morty Sklar, Editor & Publisher
P.O. Box 1585, Iowa City, Iowa 52244
(319) 338-0041

MEN & WOMEN
Together & Alone

EDITED BY MORTY SKLAR & MARY BIGGS

previously unpublished
poetry, photographs and paintings

The Spirit That Moves Us Press

Iowa City : 1988

Acknowledgements

We gratefully acknowledge a grant from the National Endowment for the Arts, in partial support of this collection.

Gratitude is also expressed to the following for their show of support in cash or services: Helen and Phil Kahn, Peter and Dorothy Rinaldo, Norma Vogel, Ann Struthers, Jim Gilmore of Zephyr Copies, Walt Ellinwood, John and Maggie Hesse, and Charles L. Eble.

First U.S. Edition
This book is issued also as Volume 9, No. 1 *The Spirit That Moves Us.*

800 Smyth-sewn clothbound (including an A-Z signed edition) & 1800 trade paperbacks—all printed on acid-free paper—were manufactured in the U.S.A. in August 1988.

The Spirit That Moves Us is indexed in *The American Humanities Index, Index of American Periodical Verse* and (some issues) *Granger's Index to Poetry* and *Poetry Index Annual* (Roth Publishing).

Library of Congress Cataloging-in-Publication Data:

Men & women : together & alone / edited by Morty Sklar & Mary Biggs. -
- 1st U.S. ed.
    p.   cm.
   "Also issued as volume 9, No. 1 of the Spirit that moves us"—
  ISBN 0-930370-29-5 (alk. paper) : $12.75. ISBN 0-930370-30-9 (pbk. : alk. paper) : $7.00. ISBN 0-930370-31-7 (signed A-Z : alk. paper) : $25.00
   1. Interpersonal relations—Poetry. 2. Men—Poetry. 3. Women-
-Poetry. 4. Poetry, Modern—20th century. I. Sklar, Morty, 1935-
. II. Biggs, Mary. III. Title: Men and women.
PN6110.I57M46 1988
808.81'9353—dc19   88-18333
                                    CIP

Preface

As with other thematic collections from The Spirit That Moves Us Press, *Men & Women* was announced as a title in our open solicitation of manuscripts; we did not impose guidelines on potential contributors—other than to say that we weren't focusing solely on romantic or male-female relationships. Of course, once we chose the works we were to include, we thought about how to place them—grouping by subject or style—but this was done organically, avoiding section headings. Headings look neat but give the reader a false sense of simple order and finite possibilities. Besides, many works could easily fall under various headings, so why pigeonhole them? A case in point is the poem, "Coming Out," by Laurie Kuntz: Mary thought the characters in the poem were women; Morty thought they were woman and man. So under what heading would that poem fall? Its focus of interest is the changing of a relationship—the kind of change to which people of any sex or sexual preference can relate.

Choosing a title was tricky, and we don't feel we came up with the perfect one, if indeed there is a perfect one. Originally, the subtitle was *Together & Apart*, but that seemed to suggest relationships where people were apart from each other. *Together & Alone* seemed to alleviate that problem somewhat, but perhaps suggested that *alone* is necessarily a negative state. We wanted poems of aloneness that expressed satisfactory, as well as unsatisfactory, relationships of people with the world, and with themselves.

Our cover photo, by Doug Smith, is an absorbing and somewhat ambiguous expression, but also does not seem to say all that we wanted to convey about this collection; but the fact that what this book expresses as a whole cannot be summed up in its title or cover art is why we did it in the first place. So we'll just take comfort in the saying, "You can't tell a book by its cover," and in our expectation of your finding the work within, various, enjoyable, and stimulating.

Mary Biggs dedicates this book to
the women who have been close to her.

In Memory of

Jaroslav Seifert
Darrell Gray

Contents

8

Linda M. Hasselstrom
THE BLIND CORRAL

Along the highway to Canyon de Chelly,
four Navajo boys ride ponies,
driving a galloping herd of horses:
blacks, sorrels, paints.
The colts canter, nosing their mothers' flanks,
unaware of the trucks and saddles waiting,
the cold bits, the bridles.

Other horses graze hilltops,
unaware of their grace. The wind
wraps fine tails around slender legs,
ripples shining manes.
Horses doze in the sun,
never looking at fences.

Down the halls of each school
in the land, young girls caracole and prance.
Long clean hair brushes their shoulders,
their faces are open as meadows,
eyes clear and trusting.
Fearless they buy eye shadow, rouge
to cover the fine bones of their cheeks
with false blushes,
to ring their eyes with color.
They force their firm breasts higher
into nets of cruel wire.

AFTER THE STORM

I climb the ladder, shakily as usual, to see if the wind
tore off more shingles, or pounded more holes.

11

Up on the roof I can see clear
to the next ranch, the Badlands—and no further.
I can't tell how the Supreme Court will rule,
if the famine will get worse, or the war go on.

Birds eye me with alarm. I can't hear the telephone
if it rings. The car and its engine trouble are too tiny
to bother me. The garden needs weeding, but I can't see weeds
from here—only a green rustle of corn, a swirl of squash vines,
bulges of orange pumpkins. The cat stalks a mouse in the grass,
unaware I'm watching. The air is pure, the wind fresh,
filled with strange voices.

A bird alights on the chimney, cocks his head,
queries, then ignores me and sings. Another
swoops by my head, chuckling.
It will soon be dinner time, but who can cook
on a roof? I can't answer letters, or vacuum the living room,
or worry about unpaid bills. There isn't a single thing
I should do
that I can do
up on the roof.

Mike Delp
AMERICAN MALE

for Jack, Nick and Terry

It goes back to railroads, maybe before.
Getting up a head of steam then taking
the rise out of each grade,
each wheel massaging the tracks,
wearing them down,
a matter of friction,
the land giving way,
then the long curves,
the engine working against gravity,
and the trestles shaking
all the way to bedrock,
the water cutting through six inches
of creosote,
and the jackhammers singing,
spitting steam,
the smell of sweat and steel,
a man's arms sending each spike
against the grain.

So we pack it in,
the wilderness falling away,
the rails torn up,
railroad yards full of ghosts,
and behind our backs
we listen to the sound of rotting timber,
some force loose in the world,
shutting trunk lines,
turning cabooses into dress shops,
whole trains into shopping malls.

* * * * *

Generations of fathers,
grandfathers, sons and brothers,
wars, fights, each killing going deeper
into the bone,
while out in the back,
near the spot where your grandfather told you
he first made love
the lilac thickens, grows wild,
always blooms the whole summer.

* * * * *

My hands know the tools,
know how to fix cars, run a saw,
how to pull a line tight in the middle
of a river,
know how to stack wood for the best fire,
have caressed countless knives,
fishing hats, fly rods,
tackle,
threaded ten thousand worms,
pulled chain saws out of bone,
know how to pull a hook through the skin
to get it free,
how to sleep against ice,
how to bring a horse down with one shot
into the ear,
how to whisper the child back to sleep.

* * * * *

Your father gives it to you like a disease,
passing in handshakes,
tools, good boots.

* * * * *

Blood Brothers.
He Ain't Heavy He's My Brother.
Travelin Man.

Ramblin Gamblin Man.
I'm a Man.
When a Man Loves a Woman.
Man of Constant Sorrow.
The Man who Never Returned.
* * * * *
The dream goes this way:
You show up at the ball park,
your mitt oiled from two weeks of rubbing
neatsfoot into the pocket,
and you wonder why the locker room is empty.
You step into the light and see
two teams of women playing softball.
For a moment you think you'll protest,
throw a little dirt on the ump,
but when you look into her face you begin to realize
how the game has changed,
how you must first ask to bat,
then step up and keep the ball in the park,
running the bases as if you never really cared
whether you ever made it home.
* * * * *
You look in the mirror.
You're no hunk you think.
No macho boy.
At the encounter group a Dr. tells you to
soften up, cut your hair,
get a 'look',
stare at yourself for hours in the mirror,
learn to use mousse,
find that perfect earring,
but when you get home,
you drink a bottle Jack Daniels,
walk out into the swamp behind the house,
and listen for the coyotes to sing you back.

15

Janet Reno
THE SENORITAS

From the wide world they visited,
they came to the parties and civilized flings.
They cut cakes in the garden.
Their lace combs rode high;
they wore new clothes and strange scent,
clothes, like their bodies, flowering.
They even had veins in the silver
whites of their eyes as tiny
as ruby thread.
Their skirts were short.
They had such calves
and such stone strong feet
that the boys were dizzy and nervous.
They took it as long as they could.
After awhile they broke from each other,
stood, holding their punchcups,
close by their softest aunts.

Jo McDougall
HER STORY

I slide into a booth at McDonald's
to sit with my daughters and my mother
who tells me the story I want always to hear.
It begins with a tent revival
in August
in her small, mad town.
There is an evangelist, soon to be my father,
with Brilliantined black hair.
Standing before the borrowed pulpit, shoes buried in sawdust,
he marries my mother with his eyes.
He leaves her before I am born,
taking his Bible and her mother's brooch.

My daughters love the story.
At five and seven they are already turned
towards Araby, towards Byzantium,
they and others like them from towns
in Nebraska or Iowa or Missouri,
towns of summer revivals, visiting preachers,
the one wide highway out of there.

Jack Driscoll
AMERICAN MYTH

The night I took my son to the drive-in
to see TARZAN,
I did not know Bo Derek would undress
so completely on the enormous screen
above a field off Highway 10.

My son was already asleep when I rolled
the window down,
threw the speaker hard to the ground
and flashed my high beams on and off
in protest of what the young might have seen,
wide-eyed behind those windshields in the dark.
What I had hoped for
was Johnny Weissmuller's simple commitment
to his original Jane,
and their son, Boy, conceived
without anyone thinking once of copulation.

I wanted to applaud the decent life,
the secrecy of good sex
with the first woman I had loved since divorce.
So I carried my son up to bed,
remembering how Tarzan bellowed
on his way home through the trees,
sometimes closing his eyes in the moonlight.
If I could arrive just once like that,
the earth dancing in shadows below me,
I'd make no apologies for my hairless chest
or skinny arms I swung with out of childhood.

At forty I still feel the intimacy
of the old black and white at the Victory Theater
where I sat by myself in the front row,
often through both shows.
I whisper now, "Me Tarzan, you Jane,"
as though nothing has changed,
an irrational notion, a trick the mind plays
to preserve our stories from time.

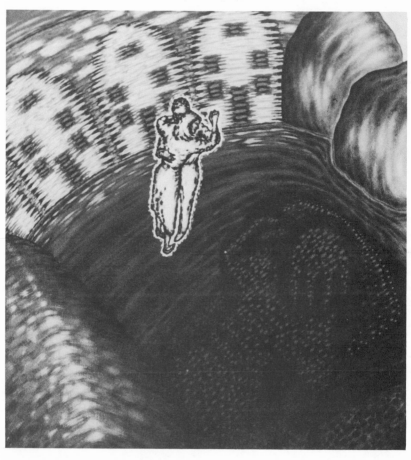

Christine Perri (& facing page)

Michael Hettich
MERCY, MERCY

Every time we argue
my wife becomes a horse.
Not a symbol or a dream.
A true horse. There's nothing
I can do then but let her
run.

On her back I can hardly
breathe. I am ducking
branches and wires
as she races down the street.
Of course I can't talk now.
I hold tight to her mane

and beg mercy.
I am a simple man,
grateful to find myself
face down in the dust,
snakelike and coiled
as she rears and begs mercy.

And I sell it to her cheap.
One bite. Then we're a family.

ANNIVERSARY

The horse in our bedroom
came in with the flowers
we picked this early
morning together.

We noticed it first
when you started to sing.

What's left of our beautiful
daughter, who rode
as the sea rides over
the sea, to another shore?

The horse is too big
for our cramped bedroom.

We will ride out tomorrow,
braid its mane
with flowers, turn it
back to the flowers.

Until then we will mount it
quietly, both of us,
here in this small room
together.

for Colleen

Laurel Speer
WELL, ONDINE, YOU'RE NOT SIXTEEN
AND LOST YOUR PEARLS

Once your only cashmere sweater balls up,
you know it's over. I worked at Kresge's
one whole summer selling ribbons and thread
to housewives in downheel slippers, painted
toenails and head scarves over bobby pins
stabbing curls. How pink can a scalp be?
Leroy Droit killed me in that sweater;
stabbed me under the gear shift. We leaked
prodigiously; we seeped, we emptied ourselves
like beakers of Lepage's. We beat ourselves
almost to death on blue plastic seat covers.
I was the biggest hibiscus in horticulture,
so lush and open he never had to promise me
a thing. Leroy had equipment, I'll say that.
Droit du seigneur, I later said, but that
was after I got educated.

Laurel Ann Bogen
BRAND NEW DANDY

the First Time I read JANE EYRE
I was 14 and I thought Mr. Rochester was grand
and of course there was poor
    proud Jane
and I suffered great indignities

   ALL FOR LOVE

but that was OK   really
   it was in the end ANYWAY
love triumphs over injustice
this may sound (all) (Too Much) mental
but darling that's how my cortex
   works
        it can explain
how we come to this place
   humbled by life
          only to find
our gothic hearts discreetly rustle against time,
refashioned brand new and dandy

Stephen Dunning
YOU MIGHT SAY...
THIS IS THE STORY OF MY LIFE

i

The dark bruise of the August storm touches down
near Blue Earth, snaps power lines and throws Laverne's
cousin up against Ed Loeffler's barn. Later the boy will
tell how the plangent wind "grabbed me like a giant,
flang me half way up the barn."

Laverne and I are safe in Faribault. We meet at uncut
fields, romp bare-ass in the wheat. We wonder where in
the en-tire universe could there be two such lovers as us.
Early Fall we sign off, take our pay to party in Mankato in
motels with tv and indoor pools.

We hear that the Feds are hunting Inez, Black Kettle's
great niece. We put out word we'll take her in. Quick as
fire she finds us, stays two nights, and splits without a
goodbye, taking Laverne's blue cotton blouse. Through
the blinds we watch the FBI pull out toward St. Paul. We
buy six bottles of Yoerg's, chug-a-lug to the failure of the
fuzz.

ii

Earlier, one Sunday night at home, in Faribault, my old
man's band drinking beer. Arn Bower says, "Man, we
don't even got us a name."
Les Bruch says, "Well, we're only six fat Dutchmen."
"Oh yass!" the old man says, holding up his Yoerg's.
"That's us! The Six Fat Dutchmen! For sure." He leans and
says so everyone can hear, "Don't never drink water, fish
fuck in it, son."
I'm embarrassed, but never forget.

iii

I take the job in Blue Earth, raking cans. That
Christmas Eve, Green Giant 2, Arn Junior puts his hand on
Laverne's back and pulls her in for a kiss. Laverne just
flirts, she's a sweet girl but dumb. No matter, though,
she's A-ok with me, we've had great times. Yet my arms
are filagreed with cuts from raking cans. I got me two
weeks' pay. I got Arn Junior's map to Scarback Lake, a
lake I never fished, supposed to be walleyes big as
sharks. The Rambler's running good, I'm feeling carefree
and wild.

iv

Christmas Day I take off, never even kiss Laverne
goodbye. I wonder is she still in Blue Earth, scared and
alone? did she parlay her smile and flirty eyes into more
than what her parents had for thirty years? did she keep
her derring-do? find herself another sweet man like me
—a wanderer, pockets hot with cash?

v

It ends up Maria and me in Grand Forks, where the
wind lives west of town near Malt-O-Meal and smells at
night like fresh-baked bread. We learn we cannot hear
the siren wail—our son says *while*—when great winds
wrap around the town and topple silos and trees.
Maria says, "Our crew's ok, but this town lost its mast."
Maria's Filipino, says she cannot stay and hear that
mayor speak to the Fourth of July.
So off we go, heading west. We hear Doris Day sing

27

"Que Sera Sera" maybe 1000 times. Past San Juan
Capistrano we buy dishes and a red dragon kite from a
tall man on the beach and drive to where we will live but
never leave unscarred, where our chickens finally hurl
themselves into the scarf of traffic on Camino Real.

"The dishes are so beautiful," Maria says, "will it last,
do you think?"

"Talk right," I say. "People here care what you say."

IonunIonunIonunIonunIonunIonunIonunIonunIonunIonunIonun

Uni
UnionUnionUnionUnionUnionUnionUnionUnionUnionUnionUnion

M. R. Axelrod

Julia Alvarez
THE WEEKEND

Before you round the corner and are gone
I wave and note how easily my palm
blots out your car. The motor's hum
merges with Sunday traffic back from church.
You drove up for a weekend visit
to give my life a closer reading,
then catch me up on your story:
both plots, this time, going well,
the heroines about to make big moves
we hope will end with love.

If not, that's what we're friends for:
late nights or weekends when the rates
go down, we call and splurge on sadness,
bad dreams, or good intentions that become
ambivalent in deed, desires to be saved
in some big way we've learned about in the movies.
Always, we bring up love, either in its past tense
as loss or in its future, longing...
Between loneliness and goodbye, we meet
and call it since we're women, *friends*.

Before you left, we wept, promised absolutes
we hope we won't be called to account for
midweek when we're hard at work
earning the living heroes used to pay for
when we were heroines of our mothers' stories.
Back in my house, recovered, I fold your bedding,
roll the mattress back into the couch
and tidy any little disorder you created
by being here...ashamed I've saved my heart-
breaks for the men who come and go.

Laurie Kuntz
COMING OUT

The day you told me,
you were making bread;
there was only that smell
of baking in the room.
I tried to move words
around, make them right,
as if what you were
had never been named.
Gay, your voice a sound like
something that is almost silent.

With the two of us
there was always that comfort:
"A good loaf calls for a sense
of timing," you said,
and slapped dough into bread.
As I pushed the blond strands
out of your eye your hands
were kneading, punching deep
for the last rising.

for K. P.

Michael Andrews (& facing page)

Lowell Jaeger
WHERE WE WENT WRONG

An old story. In the movie
the scientist brings the deadman
home, stretches him like so much dough
on the workbench and puts a lifetime
of wires and switches and willful miracles
to work. At first the deadman only breathes.
Then sure enough the scientist coaxes him
to speak, teaches him what to say.
The limbs are useless on their own
but with loving manipulations the scientist
stirs them into simple gestures
of an almost normal daily routine.

Trouble is, the deadman never learns
gratitude. He becomes a sort of monster,
arrogant, self-righteous and condescending,
just like you called me. I wanted to love you
like a savior, a mother, a queen.
I wanted to be handsome and faultless
as the superman you fashioned me to be.
By the time you had restrung the broken segments
of my spine, healing nerves over
the splayed ends of my divorce, I wanted
to serve you for whatever purpose you named.

Till one day even lying beneath you
a tiny voice called out in me like a soft,
convincing alarm. I remember
waking up that morning surprised
I had things to do, errands to run on my own.
I'll never forget the monstrous debt
I owe you, the wide screen horror

in your eyes, the accusations of betrayal
you spit out after me, as I packed
every last scrap of self-respect I could snatch,
and I went striding out into daylight,
looking to make a name for myself.

Amy Lockard
THE CONCEPT OF GRACE

There were times I thought I could go back, thousands of days
back from today.

I believed I did right just by living. But I worried about you.
You thought about things I'd rather not. Remember,

Grand Cayman Island, diving Pedro's Castle, the enormous queen
angel, the light through the sea?

You would not take grace over joy, would you? Or,

the orchard near Cambridge, jam melting on our scones and
the bees swarming around us. The sun was so hot that day.

You wouldn't. We know how life is when there's joy. It works
'til the end, you say. It works until then. But,

When I was nine I went to lunch with my father. I wore a blue
dress, and I wrote in my Barbie Diary how grown-up I felt.

Now I remember the dress better than the lunch. But each was
part of the other. I believe grace comes naturally. We had
grace through our joy.

At the end of a lifetime, like the end of a fable, you could say,
in parting, "Above all, be joyful." Most people would buy
that, you can't say they wouldn't.

You're leaning forward. I know you're going to ask, "But what
about grace?"

Sit back, then. Children are graceful, and God is.

But ... don't interrupt me.

Joy is irresistible, like light rays bent by a prism.
The pattern dancing on the wall is the show, is the reason.

And ... let me finish. Remember? I do,
On Michigan Avenue, when we danced under the awning out of the
rain, in the fading darkness of dawn?

Jim Grabill
SATURDAY MORNING

As we wake,
you touch me,
your lips on my shoulder.
I move my hands
over your back
and we hold each other,
in an hour that no one
can take away.

In longing, holding you,
I almost cannot bear
the passion I feel
waking this morning,
in the second
half of my life,
on an earth that sometimes
gives us a place to be calm
and humanly delicate.

When a morning like this
is given, nothing
can take it away.

Jay Griswold
THE INSOMNIA OF THE HEART

Don't listen to the dark pulsations that follow you
like footsteps on the empty streets leading out
past the last house with a light on, and a shadow
that floats behind the curtain like a ghost ship
carrying its full cargo of memories through the fog
that never dissipates beyond the black rocks
of those coastal towns that will say:
It is autumn, it has always been autumn,
and another boat didn't return today.
You saw it all once in the eyes of a girl
who stared at you strangely as she walked away.

And there are times she returns to you pale and afraid,
she opens the door and looks out
with all the melancholy of a traffic light
in a small town at midnight.
And what good does it do to explain
you were looking for someone?
Her mother leaned back in a chair,
gazed at you, and said nothing.

Will you see the girl now as you pass the house?
Her hair seemed to give off a golden light
like a cornfield in which one wakes at dawn.
But the curtain is drawn, and the shadow drifts
silently, back and forth across the floor
as if on the deck of some nameless ship
that was lost, a lantern, still lit, by the wheel
that will never let go of the sea.

Gene Armstrong
A PIECE AT A TIME, I TAKE YOU IN

The kid's finally dead to the world;
the dog's locked up. In their aquarium
beside the sofa bed goldfish won't watch

our oddly-matched ranges of hips curve
against each other. I remember June nights
on my parents' porch when, parting,

you withdrew the press of that same weight
and left me sleepless. Now, under a worn
wool blanket that shrank when washed

before I knew better, your mouth finds mine.
Stretched over angles of muscle and bone
your damp skin jars me again with alien

coolness. Your lips on my neck, hand
at my back melt me around your edges.
You think you fill me with glittering cities

and the sighs of eighteen-wheelers shaking
asphalt ribbons across plains where Sioux
warriors once rode in moonlight; but, oh,

a piece at a time I take you in . . .

Julia Carson
OUT OF BODY

I am rising into the whiteness of clouds,
a wild goose startled by the sound of man.

I am as high as the pink of morning.
When I turn, I see the two of us below:
a clenched jaw, a knuckled hand,
a red effort of tears held back.

We are tiny, our problems minute.
So small I want to answer an urgency
to help, to fix things up. My head is light.
My lungs, full of space. I am descending.

J. Kates
WAITING MY TURN

Where I wait naked the plaster steams.
You have lowered your body into the bath
(I listen for sighs and the lap of water)
pores open to the languor of dreaming
warm variations on familiar themes
I, from the accompaniment, can guess at
while you stretch at length, soap and lather
and rinse with smooth commercial creams.
No goddess ever emerged like you
wrapped in exotic cotton, dribbling jewels;
no queen ever stepped into the hallway
in such a cloud of exhaled perfume
as you, letting me know the shower's free:
the hot rain that falls only on me.

PLACES OF PERMANENT SHADE

Through the long light of afternoon
we go on descending.
We never made it to the top.
Where the wind started to bite with small teeth
you looked up past scrub pine along the trail
to rock gray and naked as the late November day,
and we turned back.

We had come thinking we might fall in love,
having accomplished the preliminaries—
indulged in correspondence,
discovered complementary signs and fit
our bodies into complex knots of passion.
Acknowledge now it will not be so.

We dawdled too long at the scant timberline
and will have to work our last way in the dusk.
Behind the erratics, in places of permanent shade
snow lingers from last week's light fall
like animals that can only freeze for defense,
immobile and vulnerable under our eyes.

Carmen Hoover
SONG TO VERMIN TOWN

Nuclear madness
Boytalk holocaust
Women doing dishes
in some high heeled
shoes—you want
to never believe
the man on tv
Oh beware of the
foo-foo girls
They've got
their own world.

I bumped into a man
right on the street
he was wearing some shoes
they were brown.
He said woman
I have noticed that
you're practicing
now when will you
stop playing God.
I said as far
as I know we have
only just begun.
So
I pondered on home
and there was my dad
he was wearing some boots
they were bad, uh-huh.
He said baby
I can see that
you've been practicing

now when will you
start showing yourself.
I said maybe
I just hide
me from you.
Then
I flew out west
to see Guccione
he was wearing some clothes
he looked fine.
I said Bobby
it's no secret
you are practicing
now when will you
stop spreading those lies.
He said believe
in something long enough
it comes true every time.
Sweet thang.

Nuclear madness
Boytalk holocaust
Women doing dishes
in some high heeled
shoes—you want
to never believe
the man on tv
stay clear of the
foo-foo girls
They've got
their own world.

David Hilton

"PACHUCO HOP" – CHUCK HIGGINS, 1954

That music puts you in the mood to move,
to stomp some dudes,
to close knuckles around a roll of dimes
and flatten windpipes.
We called our shoes *stompers*
whatever style:
crazed brown alligator wingtips,
purple suede, oxblood moccasins,
black dagger-toes, 'sicle boots.
All had horseshoes,
nailheads filed to a point,
steel moonslice taps
studding the soles.
We slipped and slid
on the scored floor
of our underground bowling alley,
dancing on our weapons.
Cut 'em up, blind them,
stomp their balls,
stomp their faces—
gasping chants as we jerked
and skated to the saxophone's
honks and squeals,
Chuck Higgins' "instrumental"
melodic as fuck-grunts,
no need for words
when your fists could sing.
Do the Dirty Bop—
black chinos hang
from the root of your dick.
More nickels in the jukebox
until Ingah the Skag leads you

into the poolroom's darkest corner
and dry-humps you raw
against your belt buckle,
moaning into your greasy hair
how much she loves only you
and your French kissing,
and you *do* love her
right up to that instant
you groan and are suddenly sticky
and stained and so sore
it'll be two hours before
you can whip it again.
Over your head, in the sun,
the lames are working their bagboy jobs,
wearing white Safeway shirts,
daddy's bowties,
saying Thank You, opening
bank accounts, going steady,
keeping their flattops waxed,
their shoes always soft
and powdery white.

                    2

Then we rose
from the Village Bowl,
scouted the vast parking plaza
for unlocked cars,
a bottle of bourbon in the backseat,
an easy hotwire up front.
Mostly we snuck into the Lorenzo Theatre
to catch the end of A-Bomb
monster movies—a buck to whoever
got bare tit first.

No one would win
unless Ingah was there alone,
then we all won. The main feature
was Intermission, the candy counter
where always stood Bobo (no
last name), Bobo in everybody's way
but no one complaining,
his force-field radiating
off coconut biceps,
off his back muscles straining
the green parrots perched
in the tree of his silk *kanaka* shirt,
heavy red vines twisting to snakes
that spelled out KOREA—
Bobo who was too bad for the CYA
and showed no fear in Folsom,
the king of Intermission.
Once in the Lorenzo Theatre
Bobo shouted to me, "Hey, Dave,
man, fucker, what's happ'nin?"
Sick with dread, I said enough
to stay alive. And the small fast ones—
Greg Jimenez, Junior Pacheco,
Candy Candalerio, Juano Ramos—
the fine-boned pretty ones
with delicate knives, whose speech
would flash to Spanish
like the songs of copper birds,
they all got me high and whispered
Hey Dave, man, fucker,
you oughta be Pachuco, then laughed
their girlish, private crack-up.
Big joke, but why not?

They let me hang around—
at 16 I was 5-10, 180,
a pinsetter since I was 12,
stacking the heavy wood every night,
and they saw, too, that I'd be
as crazy as they wanted,
both drunk and cool, indifferent
to bluffs, poses, jive, feints,
always ready with my stompers,
assuming my Marciano crouch,
touch and you're dead fucker.
An easy choice—I'd be Pachuco.

3
All I had to do
was carve a cross, a
cuneiform crucifix,
in the meat that bulged
between my thumb and first finger,
gouge a few sun-rays toward the wrist—
best to use
a red-hot razorblade
and immediately pour blue-black ink
into the welling blood, and let
infection do its work—
easy. Then in secret
lift the bandage, show off
the festering brand, let Ingah
and the white guys gaze
upon my inflamed *Pachuco* ankh.
But it didn't take—it healed
purple, then pink, then me,
not even a scar.

Did I cut deep enough?
Did I even do it?
I never was *Pachuco*,
and all the toughness
was only delirious fear—
and Chuck Higgins himself
was about as bad as Louis Prima
or Vido Musso, both fat old
horn-blowers who, years later,
I challenged to fights in
Tahoe showbars where they were faking
R'n'B, boozey rhinestone stiffs,
ruffles, coalblack wigs, toad-sized
pinky rings, snakeskin elevator
boots with chrome zippers, deader
than the droning slot machines—
and got myself neatly thrown out,
punched sober by a pro
who knew how not to hurt his hands.

4
But Chuck knew
the stomper's beat—
bony fists, deadly feet
fighting their own shadows cast
by low, dim-fluorescent, glow-
in-the-dark rhythms, pumping out
style and legend (like Bobo
cleaning up five niggers,
the entire football team,
stomping all our fathers),
all myth and dream except a few
real scuffles that mixed tears

with snot with blood
and maybe broke some metatarsals
and teeth but never cost
anybody's eyes or balls.
All that ended when, stoned
on nothing stronger than testosterone,
I woke up in Juvenile Hall—
72 hours in solitary
to see if I had a contagion,
then I joined the Population.
My best cellmate in Juvey,
Roderigo, was my age, 17.
I read to him, and he lit
our contraband cigarettes
on wires in the electric switch.
He got out before me.
He was gonna make big money
lumping on the Oakland truck docks.
I stayed in long enough
to hear the "counselor" one day
announce to all us assembled
hard-guys, mean dudes, *Pachucos*,
ugly motherfuckers, black skulls,
Satan's Slaves, Born-to-Kill tattoo'd
mad-dog stomp artists, all us
miserable, lonely, terrified,
tears-in-the-pillow, loveless jack-offs,
that Roderigo had been shot to death
in a liquor store holdup.
"Let that be a lesson to you,
you assholes," the man said.

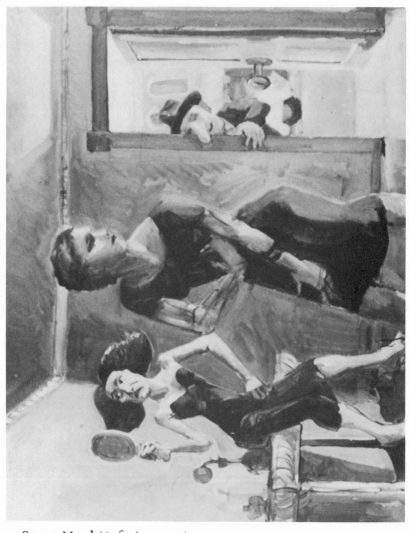

Stuart Mead (& facing page)

Debra Hotaling
AT THE HOLIDAY

Here in the locker room
women gleam like crystal.
"My husband

wanted me fat," she says
to her girlfriend,
to all of us

judging the marks on her belly,
"so I divorced him."
Out of her shoe falls a ring

she slips on her thumb. Everyone
here has a story—
an offering

of clothes, husbands
falling into bed.
And in Spanish:

"He beat her.
He drank."
Now that he's gone

the woman's
a mansion closed
for low season,

furnishings draped
with linen half-
falling past her knees

to a floor so black
and white it'd make
your heels ring.

Marilyn Kallet
THE ADULTERER TELLS HER TO WRITE HIM
"OPEN, FRIENDLY LETTERS," AND SHE COMPLIES

Hi! here I am sitting outside
in the sunshine, hoping
bright light won't stain my clothes.

That would be a sin, considering
what I paid for them. There are families
all around me having picnics, children

(not yours) in sailor suits, mothers
in crisp blouses (buttoned), fathers flying
kites.

All the sandwiches are open, and
I'm happy here in the Open Field
where you and I used to write.

How's your health?
Still well, I hope.
Speaking of health and animals,

the cat's asleep, the dog
is still deaf, but each day
I teach her a few new tricks.

Well, that's all for now.
There are no more beds,
just crickets

that snip
like sewing scissors,
and me with my friendly

open heart.

Adam Szyper

AFTER READING ABOUT WRITERS WORKSHOP AT ARIZONA STATE PRISON

They have touched my heart
Unexpectedly said: "brother
Your fate is so mild."

Yes, my confinement
Is full of movement, stars and sky
Alone I rule my void.

4 a.m., I am a free man
I take frozen strawberries
Mix them with milk
And with silence.

Michael Corbett
INDEPENDENCE DAY-nemora

It's a quiet 4th here in the North Yard.
They're letting us out in small groups, in shifts.
A fence now separates the flats from our courts
on the hill—swiftly erected after the early
fireworks six nights ago.

Shotguns and AR-15s blared and the only
red glare was blood. Crazy Convict Blood.
Four got shot, scores more clubbed, shanked
and stoned. The rec shack was liberated
for homo activity. And the world
will little note nor long remember ...

A 5%er-*God* started it. All 5%ers are God and
the white man has 999 different diseases and
was created to punish the original man, the black
man. God stabbed a Spaniard who "dissed" (disre-
spected) him in a basketball game. Then God ran
to the 5%er court, back to the other Gods. So
many Gods.

Yet the machos didn't fear God. Shanks appeared
from nowhere, clubs were wielded and God was
made to bleed. All the Gods bled. Many others,
too. An abattoir 'cause God got dissed. A
Miraculous Mayhem.

The gun towers opened fire and 400 Blacks and
Hispanics were in pitched hand-to-hand all
over the yard.   Minority Whites were too weak
with diseases to get into it. I had the

sitting-laughter disease. One of the 999.
So many diseases.

A con with a shovel had his guts exposed by a
high-velocity round that entered his shoulder
and spiraled down and out his belly as he fell
incredulous, saying before his eyes rolled back
in silence, "I thought dey was rubbah bullets!"
Someone leaned over and consoled, "Hush now,
brother. Thas jus plastic blood."

FAITH

Another Sunday dawns behind
the walls in Dannemora. Early
morning and the dark turns grey,
defining solidity.

The light takes hold and the bell
rings and the guards make their
live-count, asking who wants
chow, church or what.

In a while cells crack open and muslims
appear wearing their kufis, jews their
yarmulkes and the born-again-christians
look sharp and unwrinkled, clutching
their bibles like ammo boxes.

They gather together in silent tension
on the gallery outside of my cell,
waiting rigidly in denominated
groups for the call-out to services.

When the call-out comes they finally
talk as they walk off: muslim to muslim,
jew to jew and christian to
christian.

The tension leaves with them and
I go about my weekly cell-cleaning
in the close and blessed
silence, vacant and pure.

Jack Justice
PLEASE WRITE SOON

This photo
is from the South Lebanon
Correctional Institute.

I can now stand motionless
for hours searching
the gray monotonous sky.

Sometimes, though,
I must dive into my cold dreams
and touch your warm full breasts.

I am near the wall, alone,
looking up.
You will know me by my useless
wings.

Iefke Goldberger
LAST STEPS

in memory of a classmate

At dawn one morning in the middle of March
guards tiptoe into his cell, rudely wake him,
chain him to a hostage group waiting in the yard
teenagers like himself, older men
and one woman, who looks like his Latin teacher.

They march outside the Orange Hotel,
political prison near his mother's home
at the edge of the dunes. He smells the North Sea.
Does she know? Do his sisters know?

They cross the desolate road.
Some officer must have been ambushed again
or injured by Underground workers.
He's aware of the pattern of random revenge,
feels the bluster of northwestern winds
blowing from England. Cool hints of freedom.

They enter an alley through low dunes
paved by last steps, by hostile boots' pounding.
He does not look at the woman in front
though he would have liked to weave
his ignorant fingers through windswept hair,
touch land on the shore of her cheekbone.

In the plain they are lined up. At once
unshackled from each other, a meter apart.
The firing squad prowls into place.
Curt orders overwhelm home's tea-kettle hiss,
his sister's rapid feet on the kitchen tiles.

As the new March day opens up in bleak light
and the blindfold darkens his world
sudden fear, like a wildfire, burns through his limbs.
Then he hears her voice (or perhaps his mother's?)
against the threat of rifles, against lamenting wind:
"Courage, men, courage" echoing through his mind

Lyn Lifshin
THE FIRST NIGHT

late thru dripping
maples   the rain
gauze   streets
blacked out as a
jungle in Nam
he said let me
sit right on
this side so my
leg won't scratch
up your coffee
table   I talk non
stop fast as
Brown Bettys ex
ploding where
ever you stepped.
You couldn't tell,
they'd wait for days
camouflaged in rice
paddies, wrapped
in huge jungle
leaves. It was when
things seemed quiet
that accidents wld
happen   you never
weren't in a
sweat but still
joking. I'd
just taken pounds
of guns and explosives
off and was about to
light up then the
sergeant pointed

to the old house in
the weeds   it looked
empty shit I thought
strapping on more
just as the sun
was turning a
flame of melon
in the dark leaves
we moved in a wave
then it slowed down
they'd been waiting
machine guns   the
building ringed with
mines   even in the
smoke I saw this leg
thought shit it's mine
got my shoe on it
across the road it
didn't hurt at first
was like a car on your
pillow   I never blacked
out but I couldn't
hear   the explosion
made it all a slow
silent film I expected
would break down and
I'd run out into
the streets of Medford
late to play football

Gary Lundy
AT THE Y

American boys
with their hands
in their pants
measure the solitude
of portrait breasts,
or celluloid cunts.

this is the fiction

Boys in America
touch each other
without dreaming
of the war in
stroke and pant,
push and choke.

Lisa Bernstein
AFTER HE LEFT HER

Another woman's cry, gleaming
and black on the turntable. Then quiet
like a pillow half-sensed during sleep
billowed around her. Her legs tingled as she
walked through the house—as if she were a girl
who'd ambled home late from school,
tar popping in the heat, cars and willows
sighing past her—

to find no one there, the white stove top
serene, blue flames tucked into their jets.
All the books had promised this calm
when her fate would show itself;
the fairytale's satin pillow
delivering the king's ruby
to the peasant girl. She hadn't expected
to find it here, alone, stretched

across the king-sized bed, fingering herself
as if turning a page. Two teenagers were kissing
on pay tv. The girl's blouse
eased off her shoulders: A flash
of breasts, and behind her patch of fur
lips and clitoris glimpsed—
Night after night she lay watching,
her cry of pleasure
arriving through tears, still an unexpected
treasure, a ruby in her throat.

Carlos Trevino

Rosario Caicedo
NEAR PLYMOUTH ROCK

A common history is all we have now,
memories of cross country trips taken together,
restaurants where our babies slept on the floor
and I saw the Golden Gate from the window
and thought of home
—the unreachable closeness of my mother's love—

Years later after those vacation weeks
on an opposite coast
we are together again, still looking like a family
on another sightseeing trip.
It is the Mayflower now, and Plymouth Rock.
Outside I look at the fearful color of the ocean
and the plain houses of the New England coast.
A strong wind makes my body shiver next to his
but I don't trust his shallow warmth anymore.
I keep my hands hidden in my pockets
protected, untouched.

A common history is all we have now,
memories of cross country trips taken together,
like the Napa Valley with all its beauty
and the man with whom I shared half of my life,
his meal unfinished,
while our daughter cried and cried
in a parking lot.

When I came out
I saw them there
father and child in the California sun.
He held her tight and with a voice that could not sing
told her lullabies.

Joan Rohr Myers
TRANSITION

I am on the floor among boxes
placing the perished part
of my life away
for now. Already it is
recast into tales
tendered to strangers:
the colored beads and furs
I exchange to make peace
with new places. Old voices
roll like a river around me
repeating their benediction
over days that were mortal;
and remembering that music,
I am closing the cartons
and setting the sun
in a pink drift across the horizon.
As we turn and change
it becomes tomorrow—
one for each of us.

Robert Mehlman
STAR TREK

Ignorant and furious
At the darkness
I ram it
Through the center of you
I thought at first like Hudson
Breaking the ice in the Northwest Passage,
But more now like Dante
On my way to the New Jerusalem
Right through the center of the earth,
Navigating by dead reckoning
With only this fixed pole to steer by.
The old boys were better off
With their charts: Augustine
Clearly marked off Terra Incognita.
But I sail in night on a heaving sea
Steering by five senses doubled,
Listening to radio stars for signs
Of intelligent life,
A coherent sequence repeated,
Pitifully small against Jodrell Bank:
An ear rocking on the breast
Of numberless galaxies
Silent in the near perfect vacuum.

O answer me; answer me!

Evelyn Wexler
PARTING

In the final analysis,
the thing that really
matters, is the
parting.

I thought it would be easier
if I left first.
So I practiced
going in and out the doors,
parting the electric eye.
It worked smoothly
enough.

Then it was your turn.
I watched your back recede
like a train pulling out
leaving me
on the platform, until
the only part left was the
steam.

We learn the facts
of life:
The whole is the sum
of its partings;
The way in
is the way out;
the way out
is a Red Sea,
bloody birth
canal.

Parturition: Sweet sorrow;
Rank necessity.
But please.
Not yet.
Not yet.

Robert Hilles
A SHAMAN SINGS OPERA TO HIS BRIDE

As though a song was what love came wrapped in
a marvel that made women love men because
men were so much better at tasting the world.
Libretto or some other words coming from behind tight lips.

It might be in niagara falls or in victoria
from the hotel window where the bride can see
water, in every direction water
she hesitates there as though selecting
the right place to drown.

The shaman takes something made out of rubber
from his pocket and plays it like a mouth organ.
The bride sits on the bed as though she were sea sick.
The shaman falls out a window and flies over the water
like a giant dove, his arms pushing the sky beneath him.

The bride waves from the window not knowing whether
to laugh or cry. She is not yet comfortable with
magic. When the shaman returns she is reading a book
her fingernails biting into the pages.
She doesn't love the shaman or really care if he has returned.
She loves stories and wants to write them.

Music is what the shaman used to persuade her
to marry him and now she distrusts anything
that has rhythmn. Later she will learn to love
without her body, learn how to touch another
beneath skin and bones.

Tonight she will not sleep with the shaman but
wait in the dark for the world to stop singing.

When the shaman rises she will be gone, caught a bus
to toronto or vancouver, some place where the shaman cannot
    find her.
On the streets she will learn what power is. She will
stop listening for a man to undress himself into her life.
Becoming a bride has freed her from doing that again.
In the days ahead, she will discard certain words,
invent others to fill the gaps and if years later
she runs into the shaman by chance or on purpose
she will sing opera into his narrow ear,
his voice no longer capable of such beautiful sounds.
That is what marriage means, music the first
power that we recognize. Sleeping with someone
to open our bodies permanently.

Briseida Sancho
DEJA VU

Tex-Mex woman plays guitar
in a cafe
downtown Houston
drifts between tables
face warmed copper
by candlelight
and sings of someone
who once loved her
but she made him wait too long
now he sends picture greetings
him and wife and kids and dog

I finish my bourbon
on the last refrain
blow out the candle
and clap in my darkness

not even a postcard

A SADNESS

Please
        lie here and rest beside me
it is your gentleness I seek
and you give it
only
when you sleep

74

Bronislaw Maj
"I HAVEN'T FORGOTTEN A THING"

I haven't forgotten a thing. And now
while the heat from the seventh summer
since that August shimmers above the asphalt,
I remember her name, her flustered look and my
bashfulness. Even today I can travel those roads
without missing a step. With no trouble
I make my way to that same stretch of blacktop
underneath the rowan trees. I remember
every detail. But it adds up
to only pain. Coming at us on a bicycle
an old farmer. He passes by, and for a second
his eyes look with attention
into mine. He is closer
to me than she is. He and I breathe
the same air, the same smell of new-mown hay,
the heat dancing on this road
baked in the sun, the sun which came up today
and died. Everything
in my memory is lifeless. That attentive look
on the hot pavement, the stacks of fresh
pungent hay, the rowan trees weary
of their everlasting endurance
in the blaze of afternoon.

—translated from the Polish by Daniel Bourne

Wallace Whatley
TALKING IN THE SHADE

Sundown so late
And sudden when it comes,
Children giggling in the lane
In the dark pulling green plums,
Mozelle and Willie James outside,
Supper done, a moon in the field.
"Too low for the moon, Willie James."
"Moon always rise in that place, Mozelle."
"Too low to be a moon, that's a man out there."
"What a man doing strolling round this hour?"
"The man aint moved yet, he watching us."
"What you see a yucca bloom, Mozelle."
"I won't sit here and watch it then
Looking just like a man across our field."
"Go back in the house and draw the shade."
"A white man watching my house all night."
"I say all that is . . . a yucca bloom."
"Bring the children out the lane,
Call the children back to the house."
"Leave them eat plums, Mozelle."
"Little hard plums make em sick
And the white man watching us."

It was a yucca bloom, a web of soft white bells
On a green spine growing from a bed of spikes.
Willie James cut it down with an ax. Mozelle
Made him throw it away. And they sat out until
Late, summer coming on, so loud on the land.

Hilary Russell
THE BOY ALONE

Forest daydreams brought me backwards
to my father's fallen camp,
so I jammed the jeep through saplings,
sawed a sky in summer's ceiling,
dragged the tree trunks out like deer.
I butchered heartwood into lumber—
tulip poplar for the framing,
red oak rafters, joists and flooring.
Framing hammer, common nails,
handsaw, level, plumb line, square—
I rebuilt the camp with heartwood,
raised it up from serpentine.

So I sweep through fall—a kestrel,
hunt until the winter holds me
pale inside my heartwood hall.
Then the March light knifes me open
and I straighten into bud, swill
the run until I'm swollen,
read the year on board and batten,
bolted down to serpentine.
Forest daydreams brought me backwards
to my father's forest home.
Now I bed here, light the fires,
sing the forest songs alone.

Jack Anderson
THE PARADISE OF THE SHOPPING MALL

Every so often—but not so often
it aroused suspicion—he would fix his schedule
to make it appear he had lots of appointments
and leave for the rest of the afternoon.
But there were no appointments:
he'd just drive to a town a half-hour away.

When he got in his car
he'd feel this guilty pleasure—
as if he were hurrying toward a lover.
He tried to imagine what his friends would say
if he died on the road:
surely they'd wonder where he was going,
surely they'd think he was having an affair.
He also felt fear—a trespasser's fear—
that he might run into someone who knew him.
What would he say then?
How could he explain?

He was only going to a shopping mall;
that was all:
he went to this shopping mall—
the largest mall
in his part of the state.
He'd spend a few hours there
without anyone knowing it,
then turn around and drive home.

But when he was there, there in that mall,
there was so much. And it was always the same:
the same warmth in winter,
the same coolness in summer.

The music played, and little fountains played
in little gardens with little bushes and trees,
and you couldn't be sure if they were real or fake
no matter how long you paused to look.
The air would be pierced
by popcorn, chocolates, croissants, and fancy soaps
—outbursts of odors from the shops you passed—
and there would be stores with names
like Chess King, Cotton Ginny, and This End Up,
stores that sold jeans in a hundred different styles,
sporting goods stores with whole walls of sneakers,
and a gadget store with house fans, graters, and can openers
and battery powered flea collars for dogs.

Escalators would glide from the shopping floors to the
    food arcade
with its salad bars, taco stands, and China Delights,
and crystalline elevators adorned the walls
like stars in the heavens rising and setting.
Here was everything
in every season ever replenished.

And there were girls idling about, giggling,
or sitting on benches, gossiping, smoking.
There were cute housewives, too,
obviously glad they could spend a day shopping.
But he spoke to no one, did nothing.
Mostly, he looked;
he looked and he walked.

Yet sometimes he did buy something
as a secret reminder of where he had been,

what he had seen:
a shirt, perhaps, or a sweater,
something he could put on to summon up his adventure,
but something in a fashion not too outlandish,
so no one at home would think to inquire,
"I don't remember that.
Where did you buy it? How much did it cost?"

Then he'd stuff his package in his briefcase,
head for the parking lot,
and drive through the nightfall
back where he belonged,
the lights fading behind him
of the largest shopping mall
in his part of the state.

RAVING

Gerald died.
Dan read it in the paper:
a small item
about how he was found
dead in some flophouse.

They met in college.
Both were poets.
Both wrote free verse.
But Dan stayed on to teach
while Gerald took
job after job,
when he worked at all.

Dan got married.
Gerald was a drunk.
Dan used to wear a tie to class,
then things loosened up:
now he wears a turtleneck.
Gerald wore grimy chinos.
He was famous for raving.
He'd rave at readings
until they kicked him out.
Then he raved in bars,
and then in the street.

Neither wrote much.
Gerald was too busy raving.
Dan was busy
with his courses,
his family.
He loves teaching,

he loves his wife and kids,
yet somehow he regrets something,
he sometimes feels
his life lacks some dimension.

Now Gerald is dead,
dead in a flophouse.

Dan wonders
if he should start raving,
if he missed out by not raving,
if he should rave at least once,
just to have raved
at the edge of despair,
at the brink of the absurd.

He goes to a bar
down by the tracks
where nondescript men
watch a ballgame on television.
He has a few drinks.

The bar is a dump.
The ballgame is dull.
He has a headache already.
The men give him this funny look.
So he wonders
should he rave now.
But he doesn't know how.

He walks home,
mumbles something about drinking.
His wife gives him a funny look,
just like those men.

Elaine Mott
PLANTING BY MOON SIGNS

On television the heavy forms of astronauts,
cumbersome and softly padded like snowmen:
they spoke of the blue and green spinning planet
hung in a web of cloud—the first mystical glimpse
of earthrise as seen from the moon.
With their huge gloved hands they sifted moon rock
and the sand of another world that we could only dream about,
but never touch.
At night with my husband, I looked out the window
at the hushed lawn flooded with moonlight,
silver cushions and white lawn furnishings ghostly, floating
in the smoky light from another world.
Everywhere dense bushes were huddled together
like the flanks of sleeping animals dusted with snow.
We slipped out of our clothes and joined the luminous landscape.
The hair of his body threaded through my fingers,
his body shone like an opal.
He led me to the gate, the lantern of a planet circling overhead,
then into the garden
where each flower cup held a pool of moonlight
as if a bead of liquid mercury rested there.
The bouquet of white peonies he gave me unfolded,
dropped its petals silvered with light.
We followed the path down to the rows of dark furrows—
the packet of seeds in his hand
as we looked up to the ancient mysterious face of the moon

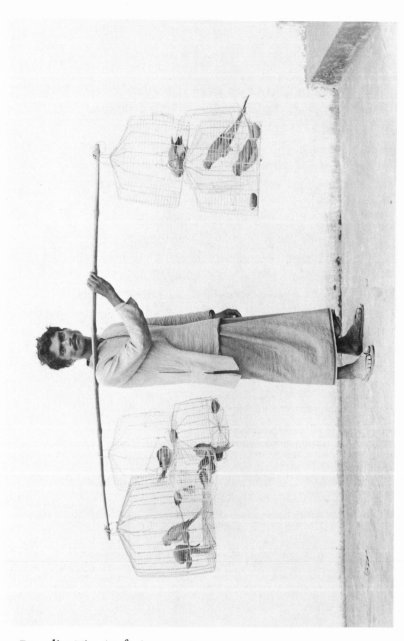

Benedict Tisa (& facing page)

Tam Lin Neville
MUSE IN A BAY WINDOW

For days I stay somewhere to the north,
eating and sleeping in spare sunlight
on the floor of a rented apartment,
drinking wine milder than water.
Even so, when I go to the supermarket
I become disoriented and feel compelled
to cling to a pile of pineapples
until the girl who weighs the vegetables
leads me to the door,
slipping an overripe avocado into my pocket
as she says, "Goodbye, and don't come back alone."

When I get home
I put the fruit in the empty refrigerator,
kick off my shoes
and lie on the floor in the light of the window.
When the knock comes
the lines I'd carefully learned
take a giddy turn and dissolve.

                    *   *   *

We stand in a window without curtains.
Late February, the winter sun is tinged with
    new warmth.

My mind moves over everything,
quick and greedy as these northern squirrels,
but your voice
has an awkward grace that slows.
So. Your length is here before me,
unbending, clothed in woolen suit and tie.
There is strain in an over-rehearsed scene.

86

I wonder whether your mind, like mine,
has returned to this one
often, over the years.
Your answer is the first kiss,
which I refuse.
I'm waiting for the sun
to go over the wind.

Your look is stern
but with a gleam of approval
for my refusal to begin.

Outside, wind spins the remaining leaves
and through the glass
the kiss comes
from winter sunlight.

Standing in our clothes
we look to the floorboards
where wide bands of light
quiver like liquid between pillars of shade.
The blond grain of the wood
is like the straight hair of children
which is like sunlight.
Breath leaves and returns
with the smell of another.

CarolAnn Russell
THE WEDDING

After weeks of lists and running for candles
to store in the refrigerator
because it was ninety nine in the shade,
I spent the next three Saturday mornings trying on
the heavy lace skirt to cut the train
standing on Jacquie's mother's coffee table
while they tacked on the little satin Mexican roses.
By then I had learned to live with
the eighty seven chigger bites (that I could count)
I got playing basketball with Howard Kaye
after the barbecue at Connie's for Carolyn's going away.
First Hilda, then Sally called, and then it started
for real. Frissie, Amy, Grandma and Aunt Irene
showed up in a ritzy van with tinted windows
and presents stacked to high heaven
like a magical tower of babble. And babble they did
at my kitchen table the whole time until
Carol and Eric knocked at the back door
with Gene and Darlene—me in my nightie and apron
and them worn out from driving all night.
Aunt Irene told me about her dead husband, Bud,
and cried because she still loves him.
Mom flew in on a 747 like a silver Norwegian fairy
always older and younger than I remembered
and we were pretty soon getting along
all together in the pink and green hotel,
going up to the swimming pool on the roof
for sodas and tea. When Spud and Diane drove in
with the kids, the fun began.
Walter helped tie the lavender and rose ribbons
on the wreaths of baby's breath
and we stored Mom's bell-shaped sugar mints

in a cool place. The women went for a drive downtown,
Frissie at the wheel pointing out this and that
until they got around to getting to the Hinky Dinky
and buying different colored juices for the punch,
cream cheese, chives and tiny cans of shrimp
for the cut-out cocktail sandwiches Olivia Diamond
made for all the Catholic weddings in Bozeman.
Jennifer showed up just in time on the greyhound
with a borrowed pale pink linen suit and a lace blouse,
her make-up bag and electric curlers
to take over the problem of beauty. And Mary
Meehan, whose only living grandma was married
three times (which is how they got the Irish
in with the Italian) drove down in a two-door Olds
with a tape deck full of Elvis Costello.
After bubble baths and posing in terry cloth robes
in front of the aqua Victorian marble mantlepiece
for instamatic shots, we got dolled up
for rehearsal dinner: me, the bride
in white eyelet and my two ladies-in-waiting
in cheap cateye sunglasses, all of us
chewing gum and waiting for the groom.
You should have seen me walking into Alice's restaurant
like a revived hippie come home (because of the song).
I knew they'd all be there the way we want—
the cousins and aunts, uncles, parents and old friends
we love because they loved us back and kept right on
even when we're weird, in ways we think we understand,
raising the energy that would carry us.
And Michael, my intended, went around telling stories
about everybody there (like the time Uncle Richard
caught those guys trying to steal the log-splitter)

and we had a toast of red wine and beer
before tasting the homemade apple crumb muffins
and fritters that were part of the reason we came.
It was the first supper. You know, the one
before any of time's tricks or betrayals
and I was in white, the color wheel whirling so fast
it seems all one circle
though you know the pie-shaped pieces
are really there—the deep blues and reds
the pure yellows and green
and that one day we'll be able to look
through them all at the same time
like a church window
and reconstruct this moment
because we'll both be moving that fast
around in love toward the end
of August, then the glare of Indian summer
harvest into the white glove
of snow where, fanning open like angels
in the perfect drift
will be the live, warm bodies of our love
sparkling with icy flakes
and even then still singing out
the carols of our names.

Marianne Wolfe Waldman
QUILTS

The best
are held with ten even stitches
to the inch, pieced from dresses
worn in childhood: ginghams, plaids and florals.

Morning light bathes the back room of the meeting house,
Lost River, Virginia.
Here the women gather—the widows, the gossips,
the brides—to work

bright patches of color
into perfect squares: Flying Geese, Melon Patch, Moon
Over the Mountain, softened
by so much white.

This one for Sarah
at the far end of the frame, sunlit,
glowing. She thinks of the man she will marry
Saturday at dusk,

imagines his large hands—washed
from a day in the mine—turning back the scalloped edge;
the familiar faces, the glistening thimbles,
no longer at their task.

Kathleen Spivack
THE DOUBLE WEDDING RING QUILT

When they exchanged wedding rings
did they know
it was only the start of sorting
through work baskets of "why"
and "what it all means," a ragbag
of eye-strain and piece work?
Now, seventy-eight and seventy-five,
they hold the quilt between them
as you snap their photograph.

It scalloped their bed
that first night he brought her
home, they tell you; covered
that winter the kids got so sick;
full moons when she couldn't sleep &
he brought warm milk upstairs;
the year the Wahoosac Mill closed;
evenings he came home after midnight
and she didn't ask; the time
their oldest girl "got caught"
with Harry Benson; memories,
and happy ones as well:
wedding rings, closed
circles, how they twined,
too hot, awake, and, honey,
holding through damp nights
he told her all his
dreams and she agreed.

Did you think they would ever
become fashionable, old quilts,
pale remnants fading here,

stitched by some village spinster
on a back road in Vermont,
whole townships of clothing fragmented
yet holding together somehow?
Did you understand
their quarrels meant nothing
in the end, that the pastel
wheels on the bed would last
longer than they, that in clear
sunny air they would lighten
into thin shades of themselves
and that the double-wedding-ring
quilt, tattered inheritance,
would flatten deckle edges
in your own white city room?
"It belonged to my parents,"
you will explain.

Joan Liffring-Zug (& facing page)

Ken McCullough
COLLETON COUNTY, S. C.
(In memory of John Beecher)

for Pamela

Heat sends the children
under the shot porch, where
it smells of cucumber.

This winter, the hen house
went for fuel. In the dust, the lone
survivor catches locusts.

Amen! Ole!
Blue jays prate and
the figs hang ripe and luscious.

Down to the last woman, the town
listens. An opaque hand
settles on a fist.

As the kudzu thickens, skies
grow empty. That is why
each one of us is holy.

And your eyes, how they
make faces turn. Twelve years ago
I thought them stark. And simple.

I did not like simple, then.
Now it fascinates. I circle
in on it, to nest.

Is our new son squawling?
This April, he kicked
enough for triplets.

Around here, they don't
hang anyone, anymore. Even I
have come to equilibrium.

You at the center, the
days move from fallow
to full and back.

Susan Fantl Spivack
LOVE IS A FORM OF VICTORY

The red that leaps from rock to tree,
cardinal,
power of choice.
The day you cried real tears
I followed your desire
cell to cell along your skin,
my face guide to your sensation,
until I took you in
and found myself
around your ancient form.

Our mothers taught us
this milk song, say yes,
and drink. So we thank
each other for pleasure
and agree to greed, nudge hips,
rub myself over and over your knee
as you come into my mouth,
or pushing your head down
down to me with both hands
whispering, now,
it's my turn now.

Sometimes,
these first spring days,
the windows open,
a cardinal calls in the apple tree
beside our bed proclaiming territory.
The rhythm of our sighs
brings space newborn
out of unmeasured time.
I love you best in the morning,
the clock turned to the wall.

Pamela Yenser
CALLING THE DOG

In the day I'm a foil
for you, your guard dog
chasing off strays.
I love. I obey.
I guard the gates
where I polish my bone,
quiet as a gargoyle.

In moonlight, you bay,
hunker, shake your head,
a leg, a pointer poking
fun, licking the dish,
rolling around in the bed.
Tired, I call you in.
Curious, you come.

Wang Xiao-ni
THE WIND IS ROARING

The wind roared through the sky above my head.
Louder and softer by turns,
it was laden half with grief
and half with bad luck.
An old man
walked with difficulty by my side
holding his thick cotton cap to his head
as the wind kept on roaring.

The wind roared in the chambers of my ears.
Stronger and weaker by turns,
it was laden half with dignity
half with exuberance.
A boy
ran cheerfully beside me,
his hand full of bits of colored paper
that he released all at once
as the wind kept roaring.

Suddenly I couldn't help feeling happy—
my black hair
flying and singing in the wind.

—translated from the Chinese by Edward Morin & Dennis Ding

Irvin Moen
WREN

(you said your name
was just a homely little bird)

Business as usual:
Your spade attacked weeds in the tulips
while I clipped grass by the sidewalk.
A blue Camaro had just over-shot the cul-de-sac
and spun another crease across our lawn.
Up the street, a black Labrador barked
while somebody's radio blared
the five o'clock news:
... radiation leaking from under the closed door of the
    Soviet Union ...
... another (ho-hum) terrorist bombing ...
... twelve blacks dead in South Africa ...
... etcetera, etcetera, etcetera ...
I was more interested in the mosquito
drilling a deep well in the unreachable part of my back.

Maybe the radio said death
one too many times,
or maybe the dog barked too loud,
or perhaps you didn't like the way I cussed
the mosquito,
you,
and the errant dirt clod that flipped
from your spade to the back of my hand,
but when I looked at you,
you—were—pissed.
Your mouth had that Sunday morning Calvinist look,
and your eyes broke concrete.
Not on me (thank God)
or the dog,

or the radio,
but on something in the air—far above.

The monotone death toll of the radio
stopped.
That's when things started getting weird.
Your hand moved to point,
but in slow motion—
index finger leaving your fist
like hard birth.
Appliances fell silent
inside our open door.
The loud Lab's mouth froze around a bark
as big as an apple in a pig's mouth.
In the middle of the street a red car
shimmered on silent tread.
Thought became footsteps in deep mud.
Then it stopped,
everything

but you
inexplicably shrinking
into feathers, wings,
and finally, grass clipper high,
the only motion in the world,
a beak.
You tested your wings
and were gone.

And the cars, kids, dogs, cats, insects,
even clouds and the sun
were now just objects in a huge still life.

The world was a butterfly in ice
and from this world where all matter hung limp
and silent from the hour hand on a stopped clock,
from this world where all that moved was not real,
where all that moved flew

from the imagination
you flew
not long—
a few non-existent seconds,
an eternity
perhaps...

before you were light
on my shoulder,

to grass,
peeking through dandelions,
chirping happy.

The Labrador's mouth snapped shut
as he wide-eyed leaped back
from the caboose end of his bark.

The red car didn't just start moving—
it was suddenly performing a perfect U-turn
in the cul-de-sac leaving
our lawn unscathed.

The guy up the street who used to trap cats
leaped from his house
and blew a kiss to a yellow begonia.

That was just a preview.
Folks ran from their homes with shouts,
laughter, tears until the whole neighborhood embraced and rang
like a Happy Face reunion.
A blue cop
pirouetted down the street to the strains of a symphony
a vacuum cleaner played
instead of that dirty little song.
Through the din a radio bellowed
the five o'clock news:
Russia is calling
for a world-wide ban on nuclear power
and arms.
Nancy Reagan has received a dozen roses
from Colonel Kadafy.
P. W. Botha is embarking on a world cruise in a rowboat
leaving South African leadership to Archbishop Desmond Tutu.
AIDS researchers . . .

> While confetti fell from the sun,
> the wren had become a homely little bird.
> With her feathers gone she was naked and humble
> as a washed fryer.

> But then she grew,
> inch—by—inch into her own kind
> flesh. Rising slowly
> to long blond hair the air held
> the way a valet holds a cape.

> She rubbed her jeans,
> patted her scarf,

looked around, smiled and said:
There.
She picked up the abandoned spade
and went back to work.

II
A Millenium Later

Legend has it
the world was once radiation and bullets.
Then a woman became a bird.

Donna Baier Stein
WOOING LADY LUCK IN PHILIPSBURG

We had spent the day on a white sanded beach
and that night at the casino on Frontstreet,
the Casino Rouge et Noir,
our money spilled through your fingers
onto the green felt of the gambling table
raising a fine dust.
I remembered moving my hand along your thigh,
the comfortable graininess there.

> We don't speak of any of it: how you draw in
> your breath at the hand dealt, how girls in
> green velvet push up their breasts and
> courtings fall to dust before your blind eye.

Outside in the *steegjes*, or alleyway,
counting all our losses but one,
we felt the terrible lure of the ocean at night.
That beach was beautiful, where we sat.
And that night in the dream:
a deck of cards in outstretched hands, one
fluttering to the ground, the dream
that warned: "Here, this is for you."

Chuck Miller
AFTER WATCHING "THE TIMES OF HARVEY MILK"

you were moved watching him try
again and again for the board of supervisors,
and finally taking his place
among the other ethnic candidates,
how much affection he had,
it seemed to slop over in all directions
a voice of intelligence raised
and giving hope to that myriad of gays and minorities
the people warmed to him, senior citizens, blacks, Asians
and he called to them to come out
from their closets, speak out
their true identity
the grave fear they faced that proposition no. 6 would win
and homosexuals across the state would lose their jobs
be beaten back and "Nazification" would take over
and the joy when it was defeated
they danced in the streets with a great outpouring

the enormous grief when he and Moscone were shot
the candlelit parade through the night streets
and the people marching silent
the great gulf of sadness wavering in the flames
the procession hovering, moving slowly forward
beyond fear

leaving the auditorium, you pass through the crowds
lined up for the second showing
and you see all the ones with the especially sensitive faces
you can tell in some way, some different sense of them
all the ones you will probably never know
the women beyond your reach, and the men also oriented
     askew to you

some of the women perhaps not so beautiful
who might have been judged worthless by the hetero sense
but most with that mark of inner suffering and knowledge
knowing the serious estrangement of
human beings who have constructed their own worlds
and burn with a special quiet radiance
waiting quietly with each other, men and women
in some fraternal cohesion
some of the men a trifle silly perhaps
but none with that look of casual brutality
Americans so often have
and most with some easy energy
and graceful kindness stirring now slightly in the dark
as they are about to enter
and see their hope rise and then be extinguished
and slowly rise again in a full measure of grief

you think of your lover who has gone over to them
found herself among them
who is now lost to you irretrievably
and all the lonely American towns they must have come from
harsh, drab, petty
each strange, shy, holding him/herself somewhat apart
probably suffering ostracism
knowing full well what it was
to be "stranger through our town"
the labor guy in the film saying
"and I probably would have thought the same way
if I hadn't known Harvey Milk, I mean that
when the cops went in and roughed up some gays in their bars
that it was alright to beat up a few queers"

the splits and shifts and chasms between us
all infernally trundling toward a lonely cul-de-sac
and I think these are the ones I should be with
but then cannot speak
and pass estranged and not estranged
under the dark trees
and think of the candles they carried
each one silent flame

something is winnowing us
winnowing us away, the chaff
from the wheat, but which
is the chaff
and which
is the wheat
our kernels are broken
we shift groping
in a sad wind

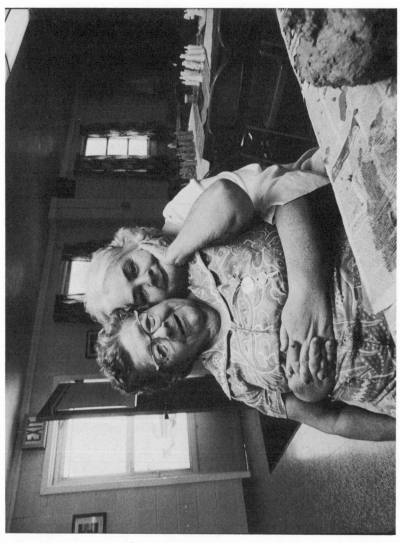

Steve Zavodny (& facing page)

Ron Schreiber
A SEQUENCE

"the hardest" (10-4-86)

that's what I've been saying
for three weeks; but this

(so far) is it: watching John
start to die, his face not so

much in pain as frowning, not
wanting to let go, his body

frail beyond simple weakness,
his spirit not yet broken,

his eyes puzzled. (why John?
why me?—questions we've never asked.)

it's like a glacier accelerating,
the town, the whole economy,

the "lifestyle" (as we've been
trivialized) about to be

engulfed in cold.

10-6-86

"how do you feel?
do you feel calm?"

112

I ask. "I feel sick,"
John says. "oh," I say

& go back to my room
to play another game

of solitaire.
oh, and oh and oh.

I don't know what to do
but wait for Lisa to come

at 8 or 8:15, wait
for it all finally

to be over, for that
huge hole to open in the

middle of my life, where
I've been filled for

years and months now,
to the very brim,

to satiety.

10-7-86

when John woke up, dis-
oriented, he said, "it was

beautiful"—not like the
last dream, before he was

ready. when he's sleeping
there's a look of peace on

his face, &, sometimes,
when he talks (softly now),

he says he is happy.
he knows he is loved;

he loves me & the others.
he's ready now.

in my dream two nights ago
I decided not to try AZT.

when I called Chip Schooley,
he called that "a wise decision."

I'm ready too, then, for
John to die. after that

I don't know anything.

hanging on (10-9-86)

yesterday he was awake,
this morning awake. he

barely talks. his body
is so shrunken that it

hurts him to move at all;
his flesh is gone. why

does he hang on? three days
ago he spoke about how

happy he was, everything
resolved, the people who

love him, those he loves,
including his father.

when he slept the expression
on his face was peaceful.

now it's a frown. have things
got unresolved? not with

me or Lisa. we are past
"ready" now & he's at ease

with us. & I have no peace
at all: at work I think

about him, at home, when I
worry about moving the plants

indoors before Friday's cold.
& John hangs on, restless but

immobile, his eyes
staring into space.

continued

do I want him to be dead? (10-13-86)

not *be* dead, but—maybe—
finally, to die. can I admit

that to myself? is it what
I want? how else explain my

anger last night at Suzanne,
Bobby, & Nancy, who smiled

that John wanted a pizza &
assumed that I'd go out to

get it (though my leg ached,
though I was exhausted).

I haven't climbed a mountain;

John's done that, but the
mountain has climbed me.

Patricia Dubrava
POSTCARDS FEATURING ABORIGINES

arrived today from Denver and San Francisco,
not Sydney or Perth, striking recollection
of our chance meeting in a stained glass
restaurant's greenery.
Now we've been to Denver railroad bars,
San Francisco cafes, Australian movies
and home again, you and I.
A passion for Peter Weir films
is among the mildest we share.
These two cards slide a glossy finish
into my unsuspecting hands.
Sleek black hunters crouch on blond desert,
my memory the target
of their coincidental darts.

Jeanne Voege
WILLIE, IS THAT YOU?

One more time
this morning an alien,
multiple elbows folded in repose
on the pillow next to mine.
Sound asleep in sublime audacity
among green percale tulips,
a CRICKET!

How long had he slumbered
purring in my ear,
meddling in my dreams
like some reincarnated lover.
Would compassion evoke compatibility?
Willie, I whispered, is that you?

However irresistible my snoring,
I am wrong for you:
repulsion, terror, midnight
teeth-clenchings date all the way back
to Brooklyn   yet
no urban vermin ever dared my BED!

Or, is this another meditation misconstrued.
(I must learn to be more specific.)
Granted, somewhere there's a cricket guru
supplying softer flowerbeds,
but what if signals were crossed
out there in the ether
and the wrong mantras were answered.

Like the time I meditated for someone
to show me the Pacific
and a young man appeared.
I can show you, he offered, unzipping his
photo album.

118

Roger Greenwald
I SAW YOU

I saw you stirring your coffee in the Tarogato
but it wasn't you.
As soon as I was walking on the frozen streets
my head addressed the air in your language,
thinking up a letter to your mother.
At the frosted window I saw your hair,
which was the color of your hair and the length of
your hair, though the shirt in grays and whites
was unfamiliar, and the small hood
folded on your back.
Only one person could see me at the door,
a young woman who looked up as I stared in
trying to glimpse your face, my face
tied off by the drawstring of the hood.
I saw you stirring your coffee with a small spoon
but your hands weren't yours and the silver ring
wasn't there on the other
hand you didn't stir with. Still it was
your hair, and your body while thinner
than your body was still your body's
proportion. You were
sitting at one of the frail tables for two
and the other chair was empty:
no one in it and he wasn't me.
I looked a long time and you stirred so long
I thought perhaps it was the cappuccino
that you always have and therefore maybe you.
I had a note for you in my pocket and walked away
(what if it was you?)
up the street and dropped it through the slot
in your door. What I want to know is did I
see you stirring your coffee in the Tarogato?
It was Sunday night. Or were you on the street,
watching a car you thought you saw me in.

John Wetterau
SPRING DREAM
of SueSue

Perfectly quiet
   a trout lets me hold him,

      you surface laughing
      dark hair
         blue shirt unbuttoned

APRIL, MAINE

clouds booming over
the washed woods,
blue & sun, Finn eats
chop suey from a pot
while I shave,
6 months to dismantle
the dead rooms of a marriage,
down to a borrowed tent,
patches of snow, &
invisibly, all around us,
sap rising in its own
sweet time

J. T. Ledbetter
SETTING OF STEMS

for Dolores

when you come to the door like that
I know you've done something
something new or different
so I look quickly behind the door
half-expecting to see your
Uncle Harold
from Cincinnati who promised
not to just drop in anymore
like the last time when it cost me
two hundred dollars to fix his car
after it went through our fence

but he wasn't behind the door
and your smile told me to keep looking

it was your hair!
it wasn't your hair.
what was it?

I knew it was six o'clock
and the evening news was on
but I knew that would be the kiss of death
so I strode into the room
and bawled:

  "You're wearing those slick
black pants..."

well, yes, but keep looking...

the telephone was turned in an odd way

that said worlds
if I could but work it out:

the couch and chair were the same
so I knew (hoped) new ones hadn't been ordered
as I was pulling into the driveway

no
something else
some secret sign I must see or . . .

but you were already drifting toward
the living room
in that casual way that draws a person
inexorably after . . .

the living room! What?
still there—
and now the smell of the meatless lasagna
was getting to me
and my stack of ungraded freshman papers
bulged from my pack
but still you stood by the window
in that odd pose that told me not to bother anymore
if I couldn't see that you had arranged
the birthday flowers I left for you to find
but there they were: in the long vase you liked
the vase that never held anything but a long column
of air
the vase from the student art show we went to
in the driving rain that night we made up
after the big one

it was the flowers

and now you waited
in the semi-darkness of the cold room
watching me try to embrace the flowers
wondering how to say it
how to arrange the words that would bring you joy
that would fill the room with fresh sounds
of thanks for this setting of stems, so,
and not another way

but the darkness caught us—
and I remember the last light in your eyes
your body arched against the window
where the bougainvillea rustled against
the cooling glass

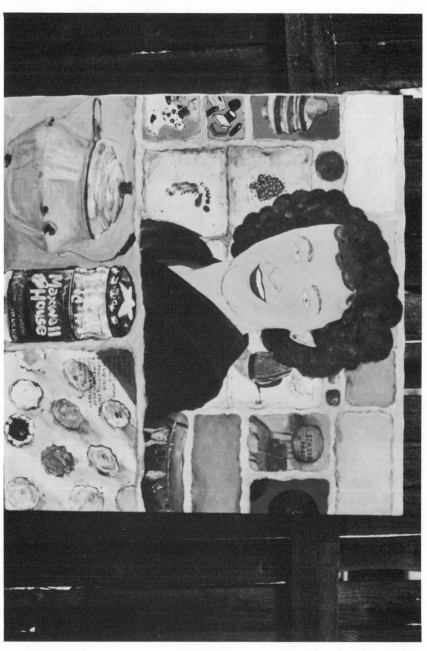

Cat Doty

124

Michael Lee West
MAKING GRAPE JELLY IN AUGUST

We gather grapes in the afternoon
picking and discarding woody branches.
Beneath the arbor, sunlight compresses
into pinpoints through pauses in the vines;
grapes swell toward it.

Deep concord smells rise,
stain the edges of my nostrils,
as I follow you into the kitchen.
I stand at your elbow,
amazed at your care in pinching stems,
mashing cooked grapes through the sieve.
Your fingers stain purple;
I imagine the veins along your hands
are vines feeding bulby extremities,
and two guarded grapes between your thighs.

You add honey and pectin,
stir the purple liquid until it boils.
Your smile is full of accomplished domesticity
as you ladle hot jelly into wide-mouthed jars.
We stack glass containers in the window,
blushing the kitchen violet
in the last hour of daylight.

You yawn, having exhausted yourself making jelly
so you won't have to make love to me.
As you climb the stairs,
you turn toward the window,
looking beyond me.
Your eyes reflect disciplined rows

of clean purple jars.
As I reach toward you,
my hands tremble;
they are not innocent,
they are not purple.

Lisa Zimmerman
VISITOR

Twelve days you stayed here,
your pain in scarves draped
around you.
Smoke from your thin cigarettes
clings to the furniture
as if you are still exhaling
ribbons of disappointment.
You arrived so hard, so
dangerously thin.
I wanted to mend you,
the fractured marriage, withered
buds of children.
I wished to see you
fat and simply
happy.

Today I launder sheets, hang them
on the line, floral sails flapping
all afternoon.
I bring them inside, stiff
with hot dry wind.
In your vacant room only the bed
stripped clean,
long slivers of sunlight,
flecks of ash
on the table.

Joan McIntosh
UNCOUPLINGS

Seems strange now meeting
in threes or fives.
Necessary
to rearrange the landscape
move that tree
allow some light
on this circle or triangle
of chairs.
Chinese geometry favors
the odd-numbered party. Even so
I hesitated in the Chinese shop
over buying the 5-cup set.
Missing faces blur and shift.
Garden shadows accent different planes.
Mistiness, scent, profusion.
How often we've met in the garden.
Like butterflies—flowers with wings—
our words flutter, hesitate,
veer and double—bright patterns
above the grass.
Not everything is possible
but this is possible: this meeting,
each lifting then setting back
the handleless cup, noting
the fragrance of the tea.

Peter Desy
HOW WE ENDED

After the forgettable movie
we said nothing on the way home
as we passed the shops on Main Street,
glancing at the storefront mannequins
dead in the moonlight, bugs
circling above our heads
in the late July heat.
Did we do this once
or a hundred times? Details
never vary in our selective,
telling memories, the brain's emblems
of our lives, sure as dreams.
The mind can't hold the shape of things
or the long trajectory
we must have traveled down.
But were there moments we could
have grasped and turned, wrenched
a new direction? Remember that summer
giving up on the garden, the encroachment
of weeds slowly—daily—invading
and sapping our resolve,
and it was only early June, the days
still growing longer.

Marian Olson
COYOTE LOVE

I wanted to write you a love poem,
but all I could think of was tacos
and beans lying flat as a plate
in my gut since last night, and I
knew this poem was going to be trouble
like you from the start in your
rusted red Fiat with no bucket seats,
picking up tickets as easy as chicks
anywhere, any time, and then
letting them fly like a fart, and
our lives blowing crazy as tumbleweeds
scratching the sand into clouds
across deserts we've foraged so often
and long where one as easy as two
can walk or run alone on this trail
we've marked, my coyote, my love.

THE VIGIL

There is no movement, not a sound
Across this sere and silent land
Where snowflakes tumbled
To the ground all day,
Like plumules broken loose
From worn out pillow casings.

Inside, the fire snaps hot,
Smoke twisting up the chimney flue
To drift outside and float between
The tree limbs laced with ice,
Their branches brown against
The white of earth, the cataract of sky.

In the silence of this longest night,
Pine boughs crack like memories,
Yielding to the drifts of snow, and
I do not know if my grief is for you
Or for me, or the world we knew, buried
Like the earth beneath the snow tonight.

Sharon Doubiago
THE OTHER WOMAN

Mornings I wake deep inside her.
But we have never met.
Perhaps it was her
I passed just now
in the street.

She knows me. I am the past
he cannot leave. In the city
her friend says when we are introduced,
you are his wife.
For the first time I accept.
Yes. I *marry* him.

I wear on my right hand
the gold band he found
along an Alabama highway
the Christmas I made him leave.
Even then I wore it on the wrong hand
until that first time
he found someone else.
When he came back I told him
I'd thrown it in the sea.

Everyone says she looks like me.
The short explanation he left me with,
she looks like you. Only
dark. Mornings I wake
deep inside
a dark woman.

Her husband follows me. These days
I say yes to everything that confuses me.

From the bed he shows me her photograph.
I am bound now to the fat part of leg
that showed that day in Mexico
so like my own leg.
And the question
she is asking him.

I meet her son. In his round blue face
at the cabin window I see the face
of a woman who looks like me.
A dark blue face in the crowd
at the dance last month.

Last month.
When we started home, north across the river,
he was telling me something. Something important.
At the end of the bridge, turning west, *Oh,
ghosts! Hosts of regrets!**
I don't want to be
the woman who answered.

Her face is in the sheep by the road.
Her body is the cypress that flares across the bluff.
Down in the coves where the sea dies so violently
I am made to know why

he loves her.
Not me.

*John Berryman

Julie Parson
SONG FOR THE UNFAITHFUL HUSBAND

"so I made up a song that wasn't true.
I made up a song called Marriage."
—Anne Sexton, "Interrogation of the Man of Many Hearts"

You drive home to your wife
in a car with no brakes

skin with the smell of rain
skin that comes close as sleep
skin beyond reach
amnesiac skin
like a room with no door
you have already entered
singing good-bye
                good-bye
                        good-bye.

Familiar
as a bar full of friends
is all you can see
have another
beer
dream
of rain falling like
pomegranate seeds
knot your tie
tighter
at last call tell them
good-bye
        good-bye
                good-bye.

134

You have kisses
homeless as pigeons, kisses
public as graffitti, kisses
stranded like cars by the road.
You have kisses arriving
like cops to the scene
like a waitress with food
like a bus in the rain
like *yes* or *forever*
too soon
or too late

hear the notes, sweet
and jagged
of windowglass singing
                    good-bye
                              good-bye
                                        good-bye.

Madeline J. Tiger
FORGIVING THE HUSBAND

"maybe in a dream: he's in your power..."
—from "Forgiving Our Fathers," by Dick Lourie

I would forgive you, from the beginning—
for your curled lip, for coming with snow in your hair
and lies, for coming with soft talk and commands,
in the woods, in the parking lots and classrooms and bedrooms
and living rooms of the fifties, for the strong arms of
silence and for all those words I called loving
words that were new on my tongue and the new names
that turned. I would forgive you for calling me names,
for calling me cute bitch rich poor smart dumb sexy pussycat
good bad whore; for calling me lazy Jew anti-Semite JAP
innocent girl, witch; greedy hot cold ball-cutter prick-
tease frigid Lesbian, yours; for calling me brilliant stupid wrong-
minded fascist bleeding heart Hitlerite witty cunt; for calling me
liar thief irresistible hypocrite suburbanite smart enemy
    strong WIFE;
conniver manipulator fake phony sweet fat; evil
awkward embarrassing attractive ill-mannered earth-mother fool;
overdressed underdressed primitive sophisticated childish matronly
nag; bow-legged plain the best lay in town. Just what you
    wanted and
out-to-get-you-pinned-down. I would forgive you for calling me
    crazy
dangerous vulgar exciting destructive useless crybaby sloppy
    careless
wise insensitive and cruel. I would forgive you for calling me ill-
suited mother of your children, for calling *ours yours*.
I could forgive you these names you did call me
when you were swearing you loved me and wanted me always and
    we should be

married and when you were with me in many seasons: the spring
when we met and you said women should never be educated
said I should get a doctorate
said I should always be a teacher
and you touched my breasts and you read poetry under the trees
and you said I should tutor our children I should never stop
    working
it would be such a waste and besides, you said, I'd be much too
    nervous
to stay home with children to be mother & wife & happy little
    woman;
and you liked my high heels and dirndls, my perfumes and haircuts
and you called me at midnight and we went everywhere together

And I gave up lipstick & cigarettes, trips to Europe
& journals & boyfriends & virginity, and you called me cute
tease, prissy, spoiled, Newstead Jew, your brilliant one-
and-only wife, and stayed near me at parties in the pregnant winter
of new jobs and houses.

I would forgive you for calling me names, changing mine,
weaving me in rhyme, nursery & moon, and I would forgive you
for loving me more than anyone in the world
until the summer our son was born

                    *   *   *   *   *

                AN OLD WOMAN
                IN RAMAT GAN
                EXPLAINED
                THE OLD SISTER IN RAMAT GAN
                EXPLAINED THE CHARM

Old Nell in Ramat Gan told me the story:

YOUR GRANDMOTHER WAS A WITCH
YOUR MOTHER WAS SIMPLE
YOUR FATHER WAS A FOOL

Her head shook SHE SAW THEM

THE GROCERY STORE WAS IN DEBT
THE STAIRWAY WAS HAUNTED
THE KOSSAKS WERE COMING

How could anyone blame— ?

I should forgive you. Such plain people.
"From the pioneers."
With an *enfant terrible*.
I must forgive you.

An old woman
in Ramat Gan
fed me the end
of my own story

I wish I had seen them, the terrible
witches, the goblin soldiers of Russian
winters,   if I could believe in curses
and witches (do them, be them) I would
forgive you, if I could remember
the story, you'd be forgiven

Nell is
nodding in
Ramat Gan
nodding, pointing, un-
spelling words

What are words? I should forgive you,
exorcise ancients. But what about the child?
the child you sold   into the Devil's bondage?
And what about his manhood?
And what about his tongue unattached
and his hand clutching
across the barren hills of his Diaspora
for a meaning?

                              I forgive you for calling me names
because Old Nell told me your grandmother put
curses and made slave skulls in her progeny, but
if I cannot save my son from
the stigma of your evil
I will never forgive you

and the walls of your smug landscape
will tumble
in your nightmares
and your gut will ulcerate in the night   and
there will be   foul   drafts
in your senses
and your dream
of home
will burn
and you will fall through cities   blinding   begging
for a desert to cry in.

Elliot Richman
"THE OLD PAIN COMES CALLING"
a found poem

Thanks to Anne

My generation trades-in our lives
as past generations traded-in their cars.

Back into life again,
I write to Anne and Al, my best friends
from that other time.

Anne writes back that she and Al split up
three years ago and went to court, about
who owns what and
how much is owed:
what people in suits and ties,
who led such different lives,
fought about,
but certainly not people like us who lived in the woods
with a lot of dogs and dope,
kerosene lamps & cummings.

Anne writes that she understands
why my poems are about "regret and loss."
"This seems," she says, "to be
the experience of our generation."

"The loss of Al's love," she writes, "was the most devastating
experience of my life and
when I fool myself into thinking
I've totally healed
after all these years
the old pain comes calling."

And, no, she doesn't know where Al is, and doesn't care
to know.

(She adds, parenthetically, that she is "no longer
sleeping with men.")

I write back that I, too, know
about the old pain that comes calling
in the thought of lives that were once inextricable,
as mine once was,
as all of ours once were,
lives that once had a future,
a certainty,
the kind of joy in knowing
and getting to know,
that feel of someone else's body in your sleep,
the sharing of the thousand trivialities,
mostly about kids and work and gossip
that in the end are more important than transcendental
    visions or discussing Nietzsche late into the night
        in diners deep in the Midwest.

Now there is the hiatus in our lives,
that we try to stuff with other people
or work
or fucking
or art
until
we receive a letter like mine,
asking
stupidly

how things are,
and
we pause
for a moment
as
the old pain comes calling.

James Sprouse
THE GAP

for Andy Andrei

How great the wonder
of sweeping my kitchen floor

    a life of dust, the play
    of crumbs on the jigsaw marble

when the gap in the heart
cries, "Sweep!"

and I sweep.

William Kloefkorn
THE PRICE OF ADMISSION

Yes, and I'd have it too,
if Eldon Barker hadn't gotten there first—
to Fanny Young's, I mean,
where he must have impressed her
with his fancy new gasoline mower,
so that now he has the money
and I don't. Hell,
I can turn all of my pockets inside-out
and have nothing to show
but my knife and maybe a lintball.

Now everywhere I go,
no matter how fast I go there,
Barker has been there before me,
all the old widows' lawns all over town
mowed smooth as a haircut,
my own mower, an outdated blue-handled pusher,
collecting cobwebs and rust
in the lean-to next to the house.

As if that isn't enough,
Betty Grable in about six hours
will be singing and dancing in a new one,
Coney Island, and I don't have
so much as the price of admission. As if
that isn't enough, the Cards are losing
to the Yankees, damn that Musial
all the way to Wednesday. Where is the man's
big bat when we need it?

As if....
Mom and dad have stepped up their quarreling,

words giving way last night
to something more palpable.
There was blood on the steering wheel.
Maybe they did the damage driving,
up one block and down another,
or maybe around and around the same block,
not wanting to do it in the house
in front of the kids,
but on the other hand
not bothering to clean up the mess. Or

                maybe they went somewhere and parked,
to the catalpa grove north of town, say,
and maybe they fully intended
to talk things through, to iron out
once and for all
all of those nasty wrinkles,
maybe even to kiss and make up,
maybe to touch each other
easily here and over here,
and maybe the words went well for a while,
until something slipped quick and sour
from somebody's lips,
and all hell broke loose—who knows?

          I know this much:
the absence of money is a sore
that cannot heal.
All morning I combed this one-horse town
for scrapiron, Barker's mower in my ear
like a P-51. The absence of money
leads to the absence of Betty Grable:

and if a tube in this old radio
should fail,
the World Series for ages hence
would go up in smoke.

The absence . . . .
It's what leads to blood the color of liver
on the steering wheel.

Barker of course is the one to be
overtaken: after the game
I slash my Barlow as if a machete
into a high density of cobwebs,
oil the blades and the flat cutting edge
and take my pusher into the thick falling
leaves of confrontation.
At this point I do not know
that the Cards will lose the Series,

four games to one,
that there isn't enough scrapiron
in all of God's creation (in spite
of the cloud that will rain on Hiroshima)
to bring back Clara Mackey's son,
that Betty Grable's legs will loosen first
their grip on Harry James,
next on living,
that mom and dad will make it, after all, each
alone. I am pushing an outdated blue-handled mower
at a dangerous speed
in the general direction of everybody's lawn.

Jean Berrett
THE RIVER THAT RISES IN MY BONES

This morning the junco's call rises
through the stiff, curled leaves
still hanging onto the hickories

and I think once again
that there won't be enough time.

But why then are the willows out of sequence,
still green
on the other side of the lake?

My father once told me: there is nothing
you can do about it, there is nothing
you can do.

I remember in the semi-darkness his tall silhouette,
how he raised his arm with his fist striking the air,
just like the revival preacher.

Years later, he sat hunched over,
his eyes full of fear.

Death no longer scares me, father.

One night last week,
from a forest clearing fifty miles east of the city,
I saw the Andromeda galaxy.

This blue light left its home
two and a half million years ago.

Now, our own sunlight reaches the edge of the cornfield

and rises across the small faces of leaf scars
on the hickory twig.

Again, the junco.

For this, my father,
and only this,
while it lasts.

Maurya Simon
SHADOW TALK

The trees rush by in a silent parade
of green on darker green.
Here and there a brigade of roses
troubles the landscape.
We saw dragonflies walk on water,
pulling out invisible stitches.
Our car leaves the autumn pond behind
in a cloud of exhaust.

It's always been like this: we leave
the north to return to the south,
back and forth as if migrating
from this season or that,
from childhood to childhood.
But you don't understand.
You grip the steering wheel as we ascend
the Grapevine, glad to be nowhere
in particular, wary of distinctions.

The pond lies still in memory,
deep in the lap of a Napa meadow.
The desert beckons to me—
cactus wings, coyotes yipping
beneath burnt sienna skies.
You don't know how the landscape burns
in my throat, not as a pain, but
as a swelling of joy that has nowhere to go
but back into itself.

You think I'm too soft: easy winters,
you said once, and I agreed.
Shuttling back and forth

from our separate pasts to this moment,
I see how it is that the land
molds each of us: you with your mantle
of snow-culled desires, me,
with my thirst for oases, for lean palms
rising like maestros in the vast
untended spaces of the heart.

David Ray
SURF

When we went to the seaside
we listened all night, you in my arms
or me in yours—beat of the sea, wavelash
on rock, swell of the mothering, fathering
sea. We knew it would stop, and it did.

A MOSAIC

One night off a train in Mexico
we walked down the dirt streets
and found a cantina open
where the beer was *Bohemia* or *Carta Blanca*
and a blind man sat in a corner
playing the concertina
and when we left, not drunk at all,
only two beers in each of us,
we observed the beauty of a unique mosaic
all along the wall—made of broken cups,
plates, fragments—of willowware
and iron china and dimestore stuff
and the colored clay that women form
with hands that put up hair
or bathe children in the shallow river.
And in the flowing moonlight
this mosaic of tigers and lilies and leaves
gleamed in an ecstasy.
Nothing once broken was lost
nor denied its place in the beauty.
And now at home in our city

151

we see glass flung everywhere,
bottles cast aside for eternity,
and we ponder what the beauty
and the pattern of it is,
the daily tonnage stamped into waste,
filling our harbors, bankrupting our cities,
as if to make a glittering mosaic
discernible from somewhere in outer space.
And we think too of our childhoods,
those gourds we drank from and left on the fence,
those liftable tin buckets with moons shimmering.

Suzanne Rhodenbaugh
SIRE

I rode with the cowboy
one night in a truck was all.
The actor I had in a cold house in the country
and the philosopher-king of the bar
got round me saying I was pretty,
serving me beer. He took me to deadend roads,
and cemeteries. We counted whatever
was above us—it was a galaxy
of near-truth, hair, nights
in that late November the stars were starving,
I was alone, I was a gray-eyed girl.

The actor has a ledge of brow, a furred gold
chest. The cowboy will be deeply tanned by now.
You'll know him by his bright saltwater eyes,
and if you have this
same gulf in your eyes, know you're his.
But if you're dark and tall,
if you like to ride wild
wherever a cycle may take you,
you'll be the barman's daughter.

David Graham

SARA WHO FUCKED LIKE A HORSE

This phrase that I'd forgotten
returned last night in dream, triggered
perhaps by some horse laugh outside,
some leering of our window fan
or maybe the dissolute smell
of popcorn well-buttered downstairs.
With it came a time when my life
was words, when the dormitory
was a hive of storytelling.
I remember the teller, no
friend, incurable college
braggart, roping his audience
of freshmen easily enough
with a mix of candor and lie.
His story returns: her name
was Sara, she fucked like a horse,
and seemed more stallion than mare
clomping bed to bed, exhausting
the next man and the next, until
they were equally boys, withered
and squeaky voiced with her pleasure.
We heard there were muscles she used
only in bed. Insatiable
Sara took her place along with
Rena the Screamer and Betsy
the Popsicle Woman. No doubt
we all bedded Sara that night,
conjuring her gymnastic flanks
under our tented sheets. For all
we knew, there were others like her,
all over campus fucking friends
of friends like a thunderous herd.

At the heart of all the stories
lay a secret we wouldn't name,
even later, as seniors,
swapping our own dubious yarns.

One girlfriend in the room next door
was so vigorous in her joy
that more than once I startled
awake and yelled "Come in!" More than once,
waiting for her calls to subside,
I thought of Sara and fell dreaming.
And thought I had forgotten her,
Sara who still fucks like a horse,
for in the years since I have fucked
like a horse, and like a dog,
like a porpoise and a field
of thistle in the wind. Is Sara
responsible? Should I say thanks?
I met her once, at a party
where she was the only female
unattached among circling males.
She must have liked the way I stood
in doorways, smiling, avoiding
eyes, for she strolled straight over
and asked for a match I didn't have.
She sized me up and dismissed me
in under a minute, and I
couldn't blame her. Now I dismiss
her, and me, and the years between.

Propertius
3.24

You are wrong, woman, to trust in that beauty of yours
Grown haughty with the homage of my eyes.
My love paid such tribute to you, Cynthia,
That you grew ashamed of it,
Contemptuous of the fame my verses offered.
Often I praised your manifold beauty
With protean imagery
So love might think you to be what you were not:
How many times did I see the "rosy dawn"
In a face whitened by cosmetics?

And from this madness my fatherly friends
Could not divert me
Nor the witch of Thessaly cleanse me
With all the vast ocean.

Cast away in Aegean waters
Compelled by neither fire nor sword
Thus do I confess and admit that
Possessed, I was roasted over lust's cruel brazier,
With hands bound behind my back.
Yet see now how my ships touch port, bedecked with garlands:
I have passed your shoals, and come to anchor,
Weary of the boiling tumult—
At last my head has cleared
And wounds have healed.

Sanity—goddess if you are—
I consecrate myself to your altars,
For many a prayer in deaf Jove's ear
Rings soundless.

—translated from the Latin by Joseph Salemi

Jaroslav Seifert
WHALE'S SONG

I spent only a few days wandering
in the South of France,
but even today I can hear the waves beating
against the shoreline cliffs.

The first time I saw the sea
I was standing on the platform of a railroad car,
I gasped for breath
and in my surprise
wasn't able to say a word.

The mimosa lost its blossoms a long time ago,
yet its sweet smell
has permeated even the thirsty soil.
But when I tasted
the sea-water in my hands,
it wasn't as bitter
as human tears.

How could I tell?
I used to kiss your face,
whenever you cried.

The best time was when
the tree of our lives
started to bloom.
Seconds, hours and capricious days
fluttered in front of me
like butterflies.
In my life I wasn't worried about anything
except love.

157

With Teige we journeyed
indirectly toward Paris.
New verses were sparkling there
and colors were exploding,
whenever brushes touched the canvas.
At that time we believed
Paris was the place to live
and nowhere else.

Quickly I stroked the sea with my eyes
and a bit ungratefully
we said good night to the waves,
as if waves could ever sleep!
Even today I reproach myself
and I've apologized to the sea a thousand times.

I thought there were greater mysteries
than those hidden in the sea.
Paris was full of them.
Human hearts, roses, and violins,
each hides their share,
while a poet carries in his pocket a key
to every thing in the world
and knows the secret of love.

We spent a little time in the Louvre,
a while someplace else,
a few minutes in a suburban bar complete with dancing,
absinthe-drinking;
we stayed a while in the cemetery.

And our youth,

without any fanfare,
without any sighing of harps,
without tears
and without triumphal arch
went away.

After that life just hurried by
and wasn't worth a nickle.
Better not to remember.
But be quiet and don't lie,
you'd better remember!

Soon, in silence, I conceived a hatred
even for Paris.
Competing with the big American cities
she lost year by year
something of her coquettish antiquity
and is different.

Above the sea time was fixed
like a star.
Waves beat eternally against those cliffs,
and if Knupfer's naiads
were to sunbathe under them
even after a long hundred years
they wouldn't recognize a single wrinkle.

Mr. Roger Payne and his wife Katie
understood the language of whales
and near the islands of Hawaii and Bermuda
they taped the song of the finbacks
whom the sailors call
keporkaci.

Whales have nearly died out.
This might better be a funeral song.
But it isn't!
In its gray depths
the sea sounds grandiloquently.

Maybe we should get up,
take off our hats
and stand at attention as straight
as a lighthouse.

Maybe this is a hymn of the sea!
The kind heard rarely,
but since the beginning of the world.

—translated from the Czech by Lyn Coffin

Anna Kiss
COSMIC TAPESTRY

A little woman looks out the window:
the penny-tree starts chinking
a little man looks out:
penny-tree penny-chinking woman
they say nothing about it to each other
because one's feeding the hawk
the other the pigeon
and the mountains are compressed
the mountains retreat
suns set and rise
suns set and rise
the living feed the living
life gives food to life
there's always some flesh on the fishbones
seeds don't spill through the basket
they sleep in the one common bed
at the one common table
they call each other rose, gillyflower
the moon's on the cool tower of their palace
on its ardent tower the sun
silver and gold
inside their tower walls
chrysalid-blue
beyond their tower walls
only the penny-tree changes
quivering, changing back
changing and re-changing
changing and re-changing
when the little woman looks out:
the penny-tree starts chinking
when the little man looks out:

penny-tree penny-chinking woman
they say nothing about it to each other
because one of them's feeding the hawk
the other the pigeon
and mountains are compressed
mountains retreat
suns set and rise
suns set and rise

down turn the heavens, sunless
the sky below turns moonless down
the earth stands still above the skies
roots grow roots from roots
down begins to mirror up
a little woman looks out the window:
the penny-tree starts chinking
a little man looks out the window:
penny-tree penny-chinking woman
they say nothing about it to each other
because one's feeding the hawk
the other the pigeon
mountains retreat
mountains are compressed
but it cannot dawn
it cannot even
what was feeds what was
the dead giving the dead food
there's always some flesh on the fishbones
seeds don't spill through the basket
they sleep in the one common bed
they call each other rose, gillyflower
at the one common table

within their tower walls
the chrysalid-darkness
beyond their tower walls
the butterfly-wing darkness
only the penny-tree changes
quivering, changing back
changing and re-changing
changing and re-changing
when the little woman looks out:
the penny-tree starts chinking
when the little man looks out:
penny-tree penny-chinking woman
they say nothing about it to each other
because one's feeding the hawk
the other the pigeon
mountains retreat
mountains are compressed
but it cannot dawn
it cannot even

the heavens mirror themselves turning
the sky below turning again
the hair's darkness stiffens downward
the sleeve flares downward
the penny-tree's chinking quivering playing
whatever is missing it seems is there
all of it playing it all
I bite off the thread, my lord
I consider the work complete

—translated from the Hungarian by Jascha Kessler with Maria Korosy

Pia Tafdrup
SNOWPINS

Like the map
of an increasingly strange
but oddly accessible terrain
I followed your advice

I was fourteen
and the night vast
when you held me
to teach the dark language

Struck and caressed
caressed and struck

Until I lost myself
and could not die
until yours was the kingdom power glory
until snowpins burst
like sparks
burnt my eyes
my skin like
a rash
in bloom.

ANYWAY

Like a sign
a special touch
the tub, the sink were
always panic white
the faucets gleamed
as if they had a will to light

I was fourteen
I understood while throwing up
and saw myself
reflected in the chrome
that green was the life color
that I must love
that the senses spoke
in the body's mute flesh

should I swallow your seed
or spit it out?

I felt deprived of a sleep
but also . . . powerful
as an angel
because I could open

when the truth will out
how else could I
survive the days
now that my shadow had grown up?

—translated from the Danish, from White Fever *(Borgen, 1986)*
by Thomas E. Kennedy & Monique M. Kennedy

Joanne M. Riley
AUNT RUTH

She died on a train,
They said. She had T.B.
And she coughed up blood
And she died when she took that train.

Grandma and my great aunt Hilda
Would discuss her in hushes
Huddled together on grey Sundays
In November, her birthday month.
She had been their elder sister.
Her hair, they said, was dark.

But why she really died, they whispered
Knowingly, was because he had sex
With her when she was sick.
Even at 12 this didn't make sense
To me. T.B., I told them,
Is in your lungs.

Gran and Auntie shook their heads;
I was just too young to understand.
But I would dream of her, the young
Wife Ruth, coughing
In that compartment on the black
Late autumn train: grey-pale
And with long, dark hair—

And of the man on the bench at the station
All alone after the train coughed away
With his head in his hands, man-weeping,
Thinking that he'd killed her.

Alison Townsend
SPRING GEOGRAPHY

Two days after my birthday:
the first warm night.
With the windows open
the freeway comes closer,
but so does the weather.
In the bedroom I fold laundry
by lamp light. My clothes.
Your clothes. Clean sheets
tumbled, green upon the bed.

In the next room you sit,
riffling the pages of an atlas
through your fingers like water.
You are looking for "Whitefish,"
the name of a bay you heard
mentioned as refuge-just-missed,
tragically, in an old folk song.

You want to place it,
the way you place all things,
in the realm of the rational,
the shape of an indigo blue bay
upon paper a real thing,
something you can point to
measuring its distance
with the length
of one finger.

I do not know how to measure you.
Holding an armful of soft towels,
I come, stand quietly beside you.
Together we look down like birds

over a map of the Great Lakes.
You've found the bay, carved
like a face we both know
into an otherwise treacherous
shoreline. But it is the lakes
that excite us, those bodies
of deep water. I ask you
if they freeze solid in winter.
You tell me you think so,
though they try to let ships pass,
breaking ice up to make
a path through the middle.

I'm not sure you're right.
And neither of us has been there,
our opposite coastlines squeezing
the middle into an invisible country
whose distance floats, clear,
but unspoken between us.
There is so much we don't know.
So much maps never tell us.
When the ice breaks, for instance,
cracking free on a large lake
with a sound like gunpowder exploding.
Why the weather has shifted.
Or how it is that the light
from this lamp moves me so,
spilling in a circle of gold
over the marble top of my dresser.

I return to my work.
The wind lifts my hair lightly.

It brings salt to my lips
even forty miles from the ocean.
I couldn't live without the sea,
I said this afternoon. But I meant,
Without mystery, the unfathomable
like whitecaps bobbing on the surface
of dark water, lit for a moment
before disappearing.

I spread the sheets on the bed.
Printed with maidenhair, sword
ferns and swallowtails rising,
they unfold with us, snow melt
watering the northermost forest.
I slip between these things,
letting my nightgown fall
like a flurry of snow or the ghost
of a winter dream, dissolving
there on the carpet below me.

And then I call you,
knowing, if only for now,
that the truest geography
lies here, warm, in the shape
of our bodies that turn together
like one needle knowing its compass.

You leave the atlas behind
in the next room. In the window
the curtain billows, white as a ship's
sail scudding over open water
beneath moonlight. The waves

crash, circular, burning.
Beneath the sheets we move closer
together, setting out once again
on this difficult journey,
cutting a path across unknown waters
that name us as we travel upon them,
making up where we are as we go there—
shaken, but persistent, and
rising and falling together,
rising and falling,
each one looking for refuge
from the depths of this familiar,
this forever unmappable bed.

Susan Sklan
ON PASSING AN OLD LOVER'S ADDRESS

Strange, all I know about you now
is that you opened the window
to let in this fine day.

Contributors' Notes

JULIA ALVAREZ also writes fiction. She's originally from the Dominican Republic. Her book of poems, *Homecoming*, is from Grove Press.

JACK ANDERSON is a dance critic for the *New York Times*. His selected dance criticism, *Choreography Observed*, was published by the University of Iowa Press.

MICHAEL ANDREWS has had many gallery exhibitions and readings, and is collected by numerous libraries, universities and corporations.

GENE ARMSTRONG also writes stories for children. Her biography of Tom Brad- and a novel about depression are being considered by publishers of teenage books.

M. R. AXELROD has written novels, nouvelles, stageplays, screenplays, teleplays, essays, articles, film, music and fiction reviews, and translations.

LISA BERNSTEIN's poem here will appear in her forthcoming book from Wesleyan University Press, *The Transparent Body*. She is co-founder of *Five Fingers Rev.*

JEAN BERRETT's poems have appeared in *The Little Magazine, Wind, Sunday Clothes, Sou'wester, Mati* and other places.

MARY BIGGS, co-editor of this collection and of *Editor's Choice II*, teaches at Columbia University's School of Library Service. She misses Chicago.

LAUREL ANN BOGEN is a performance poet and creative writing instructor in her native Los Angeles. Her latest book is *Vulnerable Street* (Illuminati, 1988).

DANIEL BOURNE (tr.) spent 1985-87 on a Fulbright fellowship to Poland for work on the translation of contemporary Polish literature.

ROSARIO CAICEDO was born in Colombia, and has been living in the U.S. for fifteen years. She won First Prize in a poetry contest by *Third Woman*.

JULIA CARSON teaches at Pearl River College in Poplarville, Miss. Poems appeared recently in *Piedmont Literary Review* and *Zone 3*.

LYN COFFIN (tr.) is a translator of a collection of poems (not yet titled) by Irina Raterskinskaya, forthcoming from Bloodaxe Press in England.

MICHAEL CORBETT is a free man now. "Reading and attempting to write poetry has done me a world of good." He recently published in *Literary Review*.

MIKE DELP is Director of Creative Writing at the Interlochen Arts Academy. His newest book, *Over the Graves Of Horses*, is from Wayne State University Press.

PETER DESY has chapbooks from Samisdat Press (poetry) and Bottom Dog Press (stories). He teaches in the English Dept. of Ohio University, in Lancaster.

DENNIS DING (tr.) was born in southwest China. He has translated from English to Chinese, works by T.S. Eliot, Pound, H.D., Frost, W.C. Williams and others.

CAT DOTY is also a poet. She recently married and moved to Staten Island, N.Y.

SHARON DOUBIAGO's epic poem, *Hard Country*, is from West End Press (1982). Her stories, *The Book Of Seeing With One's Own Eyes*, is from Graywolf Press.

JACK DRISCOLL's *Fishing The Backwash* (Ithaca House) is in its third printing. His recent work appears in *Poetry, The Georgia Review* and other places.

PATRICIA DUBRAVA's book of poems, *Choosing The Moon*, was published by Bread & Butter Press in 1981. Her poems, articles and reviews are widely published.

STEPHEN DUNNING's fiction awards include the James B. Hall, PEN, and Tamarack. His fifth chapbook of poems is *Menominee* (Years Press, 1987).

IEFKE GOLDBERGER's second book of poetry, *The Weeping Crab*, was published in 1984 by Sol Press. She was born of Dutch parents in Barcelona.

JIM GRABILL's Lynx House Press book, *To Other Beings*, was published in 1981. He and John Bradley co-edit Leaping Mountain Press.

DAVID GRAHAM has two books of poems: *Magic Shows* (Cleveland State, 1986) and *Common Waters* (Flume Press, 1986). He teaches English at Ripon College.

ROGER GREENWALD edits *Writ*. He received a Translation Fellowship from the NEA in 1987. He translated and edited *The Silence Afterwards*, by Rolf Jacobsen.

JAY GRISWOLD works as Ranger with the Water Patrol in Colorado. His poems have appeared in *Poet Lore, Fine Madness, Literary Review, Kansas Quarterly* & . . .

LINDA HASSELSTROM's *Windbreak*, a journal of ranch life, was published by Barn Owl Books. Her *Going Over East*, essays, is from Fulcrum, Inc.

MICHAEL HETTICH's first full-length book, *Lathe*, was recently published by Pygmy Forest Press. *Habitat* is from Linwood Publishers in South Carolina.

ROBERT HILLES teaches computer programming in Calgary. His third book of poetry, *An Angel In The Works*, was published by Oolichan Books in 1984.

DAVID HILTON's *Huladance* (The Crossing Press) and *The Candleflame* (Toothpaste Press), both poetry books, appeared in 1976.

CARMEN HOOVER has been a U.S. Army officer and a nightclub bouncer. She's working on a novel, and a non-fiction collection about women in the military.

DEBRA HOTALING's poetry has appeared in *Manhattan Poetry Review, The Southern Review* & elsewhere, and her essays in *The Los Angeles Times* and elsewhere.

LOWELL JAEGER received a writing fellowship from the NEA in 1986. In 1987 he was awarded the Grolier Poetry Peace Prize.

JACK JUSTICE's *Country Birthing* is from Samisdat Press. He's a pharmacist and adjutant assistant professor at the University of Cincinnati Medical Center.

MARILYN KALLET's most recent book is *Honest Simplicity in William Carlos Williams' "Asphodel, That Greeny Flower"* (Louisiana State U. Press, 1985).

J. KATES also does translations of poetry. He lives in New Hampshire.

MONIQUE M. KENNEDY (tr.) is Danish, a physician, and translator of prose and poetry from Danish into English. She's published recently in *Frank* (Paris).

THOMAS E. KENNEDY (tr.) has fiction, criticism, poetry and translations in *Kenyon Review* and elsewhere. He guest-edited the Nordic supplement of *Frank*.

JASCHA KESSLER (tr.) has three volumes of poetry, several collections of short stories and five volumes of translations, from the Hungarian, Bulgarian & Persian.

WILLIAM KLOEFKORN has several collections of poetry, among them *Not Such A Bad Place To Be* (Copper Canyon Press) and *Honeymoon* (BkMk Press).

MARIA KOROSY (tr.) has prepared the literal, "raw" versions of many Hungarian poets for Jascha Kessler. She's the English Secretary of the Hungarian P.E.N.

LAURIE KUNTZ spent the last decade working in a refugee camp in Southeast Asia. She's the author of *The New Arrival*, books 1 and 2.

J. T. LEDBETTER's most recent book is *Concordia* (Concordia College, 1987). He teaches classes in American Literature & Creative Writing at California Lutheran U.

JOAN LIFFRING-ZUG has two collections of photographs from Penfield Press: *Men* and *Women*.

LYN LIFSHIN edited a series of books of women's writing: *Tangled Vines* (Beacon Press, 1978), *Ariadne's Thread* (Harper & Row; 1982) & women's memoirs.

AMY LOCKARD has published short stories, and movie and book reviews, and is working on a novel, which is in its final draft.

GARY LUNDY's poems have appeared most recently in *Clockwatch Review, The Beloit Poetry Journal*, and *Blue Light Review*.

BRONISLAW MAJ was born in Lodz, Poland, and currently teaches at Jagiellonian University in Krakow. He's the recipient of the Koscielski Award (1984).

KEN McCULLOUGH's *Travelling Light* (Thunder's Mouth Press, 1987) won the Capricorn Book Award. *Involuntary Seasons* will be published by Coffee House P.

JO McDOUGALL's *The Woman In The Next Booth* was published by BkMk Press in 1987. She has poems in *Patterns Of Poetry: An Encyclopaedia Of Forms* (LSU).

JOAN McINTOSH's *Branch And Shadow Branch* was published by the Writers' Center Press of Indianapolis. She was a career counselor. She weaves.

STUART MEAD. No information provided.

ROBERT MEHLMAN played Middle Eastern music for belly dancers, and for five years toured with a Yugoslavian dance company in Yugoslavia and the U.S.

CHUCK MILLER's most recent book is *From Oslo* (Friends Press). His *Harvesters* is from Coffee House Press. *How In The Morning* is forthcoming from us, soon.

IRVIN MOEN first published in this collection. He lives with Wren in Kalispell, Montana, where he drives a bus for senior and handicapped people.

EDWARD MORIN (tr.) has translations from the Greek and Chinese in *Chariton Review, Confrontation, TriQuarterly* and elsewhere. He is also a published poet.

ELAINE MOTT's poems have appeared in *Croton Review, West Branch* and elsewhere. She was the De Voto Scholar in Poetry at the 1986 Breadloaf Conference.

JOAN ROHR MYERS. Three of her plays have received awards from Wisconsin Public Radio. Her poems have appeared in over 100 magazines and anthologies.

TAM LIN NEVILLE has published in *Mademoiselle, Ironwood* and elsewhere, and has been anthologized. She's at work on a book-length manuscript of poetry.

MARIAN OLSON is collaborating with a photographer on a volume of landscape images and poems titled *Poetry And Light*, and is looking for a publisher for it.

JULIE PARSON recently collaborated with others to edit *Naming The Daytime Moon: Stories & Poems by Chicago Women* (The Feminist Writers Guild).

CHRISTINE PERRI's drawings and paintings have been shown in Chicago and elsewhere. She is currently represented by the Sazama/Brauer Gallery in Chicago.

PROPERTIUS. A guy who lived when people needed only one name.

DAVID RAY's most recent book is *Sam's Book* from Wesleyan University Press, which will soon publish his poems about India, *The Maharani's New Wall.*

JANET RENO's poems have appeared in *Webster Review, Plainsong* and elsewhere. She has taught writing in nursing homes and prisons. She teaches at Howard Univ.

SUZANNE RHODENBAUGH's poems have appeared in *The Contemporary Review, The Pennsylvania Review, Green Mountains Review* and elsewhere.

ELLIOT RICHMAN's first chapbook, *Blastin' Out Of Abilene*, is from Windless Orchard Press. He has work in *Sore Dove, The Black Bear Review* and elsewhere.

JOANNE M. RILEY's second book of poems, *Pacing The Moon*, was published by Chantry Press. Her work has appeared in *Footwork, River Wind* and elsewhere.

CAROLANN RUSSELL's first book of poems is *The Red Envelope* (University Presses of Florida). She teaches creative writing at Southern Connecticut State U.

HILARY RUSSELL's poems have appeared in *Ploughshares, Poet Lore, Country Journal, Boulevard* and *The Beloit Poetry Journal.*

JOSEPH SALEMI (tr.). His translations from Greek, Roman and Provencal poetry have appeared in small journals throughout the country.

BRISEIDA SANCHO has cancer. "When my courage and perseverance flag, I think of the Mets in the sixth game of the World Series. They didn't give up, nor will I."

RON SCHREIBER's sequence here is from his book, *John*, forthcoming from Calamus Books & Hanging Loose Press. John (MacDonald) was his lover of nine years.

JAROSLAV SEIFERT's *The Casting Of Bells* was published by The Spirit That Moves Us Press in 1983. In 1984 he won the Nobel Prize for Literature.

MAURYA SIMON's first book of poems, *The Enchanted Room*, was published in 1986 by Copper Canyon Press. She's published in *Ironwood* and elsewhere.

SUSAN SKLAN grew up in Sydney, Australia. She works as a counselor in a human service agency. She's been published in various small magazines.

MORTY SKLAR, co-editor of this collection, is also editor & publisher of The Spirit That Moves Us Press. He was awarded an Editor's Grant by CCLM in 1985.

DOUG SMITH is a freelance photographer for the Associated Press.

LAUREL SPEER's two latest poetry books are *The Scandal Of Her Bath* and *Second Thoughts Over Bourget*. She's published in *The Hollins Critic* and elsewhere.

KATHLEEN SPIVACK's books include *The Beds We Lie In: New and Selected Poems* (Scarecrow Press) and *The Honeymoon* (stories; Graywolf Press).

SUSAN FANTL SPIVACK tells traditional and contemporary tales, and her own poems and stories to audiences of all ages. She's published in *Blueline* & elsewhere.

JAMES SPROUSE. No information provided.

continued

DONNA BAIER STEIN has poetry and fiction in *Kansas Quarterly, Folio, Phoebe* & elsewhere, and is anthologized by George Washington U. & Univ. Press of Amer.

ADAM SZYPER, born in Poland, knew Auschwitz. His *Greek Primitive* (publ. in Israel) & *Did You Hear The President's Speech Tonight?* (Northwoods) are poetry.

PIA TAFDRUP is one of the most prominent of the younger Danish poets, and has four volumes of poetry. She's edited two anthologies of Danish poetry.

MADELINE TIGER's books are *The Chinese Handcuff; Keeping House In This Forest* and *Toward Spring Bank*. She teaches in PITS and "keeps house" in N.J.

BENEDICT TISA's work is in the collections of Tweed Museum of Art, National Gallery, Museum of Modern Art & elsewhere. He's worked in Africa and Asia.

ALISON TOWNSEND is also an essayist. A poetic essay is forthcoming in *Stepping Inside And Out: An Anthology of the Stepfamily Experience* (Temple Univ.).

CARLOS TREVINO is a photographer at the *Iowa City Press-Citizen*.

JEANNE VOEGE is a journalist and columnist. She has performed her work on tv & radio at over 100 readings. Her poetry chapbook: *New Wave Sex In Triple Time*.

MARIANNE WOLFE WALDMAN's *The Berrypicker* is from Copper Canyon Press. We published her *The Poem You Asked For*.

MICHAEL LEE WEST raises horses. Her poetry appears in *Cosmopolitan, Sing Heavenly Muse* and *Kalliope*, and her fiction in *Wind Magazine*.

JOHN WETTERAU "lived mostly in Woodstock, Hawaii and Maine, married and unmarried." He's a self-employed computer programmer, and writes every day.

EVELYN WEXLER has poems in *Croton Review; Prospice* (U.K.); *Philadelphia Poets; The Stone Room Poets* (Sarah Lawrence College) and elsewhere.

WALLACE WHATLEY has a story in *New Stories From The South: The Best of 1986*. His poetry chapbooks are *Hardwood* and *River Road*.

WANG XIAO-NI was born in north China. She's a member of the Chinese Writers Association in Jilin, and an editor for a prestigious film studio.

PAMELA YENSER's latest publications are with *Ascent, Pivot, Poetry Northwest* and *Iowa Woman*. She grew up in Wichita and now lives in Pittsburg, Kansas.

STEVE ZAVODNY. No information provided.

LISA ZIMMERMAN's chapbook, *In Places Without Time Nothing Hurries*, is from Leaping Mountain Press. She won the 1986 *Redbook* short story contest.